VICTORIAN ARCHITECTURE
ITS PRACTICAL ASPECTS

Victorian Architecture
Its Practical Aspects

James Stevens Curl

FAIRLEIGH DICKINSON UNIVERSITY PRESS

© 1974 by James Stevens Curl

First American edition published 1973
by Associated University Presses,
Cranbury, New Jersey 08512

Library of Congress Catalogue Card Number 73-9291
ISBN 0-8386-1433-7

Printed in Great Britain

For
My Father and Mother,
George Stevens Curl and Sarah McKinney,
who first gave me a taste for things Victorian

Tous les genres sont bons hors le genre ennuyeux.
(All styles are good except the boring kind.)
Voltaire, *L'Enfant Prodigue*

Architecture is preeminently the art of significant forms
in space—that is, forms significant of their functions.
Claude Bragdon, 'Wake Up and Dream', *Outlook*
(27 May 1931)

Contents

Illustrations

PLATES
Between pages 64 and 65

IN TEXT

Acknowledgements

I acknowledge my debt to the many sources quoted in the Notes, in the lists of pictures and in the Bibliography. A fascinating glimpse of Victorians' attitudes to their own architecture may be found in *Old and New London*, by Thornbury and Walford; in Charles Knight's *London*, revised by Walford; and in the architectural magazines of this period, notably *The Builder*, *The Building News*, and *The Architect*.

My own collection of books, papers, and illustrations has furnished me with considerable material. The Editor of *The Journal of the Royal Institute of British Architects* kindly permitted the reproduction of material of mine previously published. I should like to thank Mr David Dean, the staff of the RIBA library, and the staff of the RIBA Drawings Collection for their invaluable help.

Mr A. W. Pullan most kindly let me use material relating to Sir Edmund Du Cane, and both he and his wife entertained me royally when I was carrying out my researches.

I thank all those friends who accompanied me on long jaunts in search of Victorian architecture. Mr John Sambrook contributed to the chapter dealing with Bassett Keeling. I am also indebted to my former colleagues, Messrs P. Bezodis, V. Belcher and J. Greenacombe for drawing my attention to material that would otherwise have escaped my notice. The occasional remark or reference has been of great assistance. Mr A. H. Buck kindly read the typescripts, corrected many errors and offered criticism and advice of enormous help to me for which I am particularly grateful. My old friend Rodney Roach helped me once again with the enlargement and printing of the pictures. My manuscript was typed by Janet Perry who has my sympathy and thanks.

JAMES STEVENS CURL

Oxford and London
1972

CHAPTER 1

An Introduction

In the main, we require from buildings, as from men, two kinds of goodness; first, the doing their practical duty well: then that they be graceful and pleasing in doing it; which last is itself another form of duty.

John Ruskin, *The Stones of Venice*, vol 1, ch 2

In the introduction to *An Outline of European Architecture*, Pevsner defines a building as something 'that encloses space on a scale sufficient for a human being to move in', while 'the term architecture applies only to buildings designed with a view to aesthetic appeal'. It is clearly a *function* of good architecture to arouse an agreeable response in us, just as much as it is a *function* of good architecture to work well. The aesthetics of architecture involve the proportions of blocks; of solid against void; ornament; silhouette; the relationship of a building to its surroundings; the rhythm of reliefs, recesses and projections; the quality and colour of materials; the spatial relationships of the interior and of the units that make up the exterior; the logic of the planning; the detailing; and the scale. A work of architecture may be an object that is free-standing, dominating its surroundings, such as Chartres Cathedral when viewed across the fields of the countryside, depending on its size and its shape to make its impact. It may be more subtle, and Chartres Cathedral is quite different in the context of the town, for it depends on its relationship with the humbler fabric of houses, pubs and shops, and on the intricate sculptural detail that can only be observed from a position near it. Inside the cathedral, the breathtaking effects of mystery, of enclosed space and of the colours of light filtered through old glass illuminating mellow stone make their own contributions. The plan, developed for a ritual, for use by people, reflects the functions of the building, but the function would not be served unless the architecture as a three-dimensional whole had been considered. The modelling of volumes and surfaces, the setting of plane against plane and the colouring of elements within spaces contribute to the qualities of the architecture.

In the 1970s, and indeed since World War I or possibly before, we have been increasingly surrounded by non-architecture. The boring office blocks, over-heated and with enormous problems of solar heat gain, the hideous hotels, shopping centres, tower blocks of flats and appallingly inhuman housing cannot be considered as *architecture*. They are not works of architecture because they are not designed with roots in the solid traditions derived from hundreds of years of trial and error, nor are they designed with aesthetic appeal : they are boring, and the only criteria which have been applied to them are the measurable ones of square footage and cost. Shoddy materials, squalid planning, complete arrogance of siting, the destruction of townscapes and countryside, hideous proportions, non-existence of feeling, ugliness and inhumanity have been the characteristics of most development since World War II. Cities are becoming formless; thousands of housing estates are social and architectural deserts where neither trees nor human beings can grow to true stature; tower blocks of flats, inhuman, socially and economically disastrous, continue to proliferate; industry eats up lives and landscapes at an increasing rate; while noise, mechanisation, aeroplanes and cars promise to make a hell for us all. Progress, for long a doctrine, as Baudelaire observed, of idlers and Belgians, has so often been a regression to barbarism.

When Auguste Perret declared that decoration hides an error in construction, and Adolf Loos asserted that decoration is 'a crime', they betrayed Architecture, and the betrayal was continued and made complete by many who followed. The great betrayal has been the classic error of mistaking a building that merely fulfils its utilitarian purpose as a work of architecture. A building that exposes its structure is not necessarily architecture. However, a building that fulfils its utilitarian purpose and exposes its structure may be architecture, but these are not necessarily virtues, and they are not the only criteria to be applied.

With all their faults, the Victorians understood their materials, evolved new building-types for new functions, and tackled the enormous problems of their age with gusto, enthusiasm and very often with great aesthetic sensibility. Ironically, it has been the confusion inherent in Victorian architectural criticism that has been partly responsible for so much destruction of Victorian buildings, for the Victorians tried to involve aesthetics and morals in their view of an architecture. The ethical tone which runs through Pugin's publications set up a resonant cacophony that found its loudest expression in the art criticism of John Ruskin. The critical method evolved by Pugin and Ruskin evaluates a building by its *moral* worth, depending, according to them, on the morals of its creator. The 'morality' of a building, therefore, became more important to the later Victorians than a pagan aesthetic, and this critical method is still with us, for the politically respectable architect can put up anything he likes to a chorus of approval from the critics who are only capable of judgement on the basis of a man's political views. The so-called 'modern movement' in architecture was helped towards its triumph by the fashionable political creeds reputedly held by its founders, and this would never have happened had not architectural criticism thrown aesthetic and functional consideration away when it put the morals of the architect under the microscope. A consideration of an architect's standing with the Ecclesiological Society, or, in later years, with socialism, could decide the worth of his buildings.

This non-criticism has also turned on the Victorians, seeing them as ogres of capitalism; as hypocrites wrapped in false piety (remembering that religion, according to one view, is simply another big stick with which to keep the Third Estate in order); or as mere eclectics, battling with their styles. Yet it is this cowardly approach to architectural criticism that has coddled the philistines and the bureaucrats, and reduced the noble art to its present dreary state. There has been a softening of manners within the times, with a resultant loss of conviction that is an inevitable concomitant of pseudo-criticism. A Divinity reflects its creators, like architecture and all art in which there is an element of the divine. If architecture is found to be too masculine, too positive or too full of personality, it will, like the gods, become watered down or destroyed. Similar processes go on in religious statuary, for the powerful images of Greece and Rome, of Romanesque and Gothic times, and of the violent Baroque have given way to palely loitering, mass-produced holy figures, childishly smirking or gazing heavenward with saccharine sentiment. The deities, it seems, must be adaptable, and if they are not, they are demoted or unsexed.

The influence of moral, and hence political, architectural criticisms has been maleficent. Such notions are alien to what makes good or noble architecture. Just as the splendid Eros of old was transmogrified into a disreputable *putto*, and displayed grinning obscenely at a magnificent Venus or a radiant Regina Coeli, so the worth of architecture as an expression of function and of aesthetics has been corrupted beyond measure into an absurdity and a lie. Our contemporary architecture reflects the intellectual somersault. Architecture, once a proud mistress of the arts, has become a grisly harridan, leading the souls of mankind no longer to ennoblement, but down to the realms of a labyrinthine and shadowy underworld where only a broken ideal, prostrate with diminished glory, remains.

By the end of Victoria's reign, London was the largest city in the world. Its enormous growth, some five times the population of 1800, was mostly due to the Industrial Revolution and to the commercial supremacy of Britain. As the principal port, exchange, warehouse, office, and capital, London had a supreme advantage. The Thames itself was perhaps the greatest single factor in London's position of power, and the vast warehouses, cranes, docks, wharves, and jetties that lined its banks testified to the might of the commercial capital of the world.

The magnificence of the public buildings and the great London houses was contrasted with the squalor of a large proportion of the population. The rookeries and slums of Victorian times were vividly described by Mayhew, Booth, Engels, Dickens, and many other observant persons, and very great numbers of people lived in them. Victorian England was not oblivious to her poor, however, and there were many philanthropic schemes aimed at improving the lot of the poorer classes. Peabody gave half a million pounds towards the housing of London's poor, and his 'dwellings' were models for their day, when the alternative was a family house converted to 'rooms'. The self-contained units that Peabody's Estates offered were a considerable advance, and offered some degree of privacy, dignity, and standards to those who had then no other glimmering of hope. Other 'model dwellings' such as those found in the East End, in Bethnal Green and Whitechapel, may look grim, like barracks, to our eyes, but they must be seen in the context of their times. The question must be asked : are they any worse than the tall blocks of flats we have so eagerly thrown up all over the place? At least the Victorian tenements were near the centres of the towns, so that the inhabitants had only short journeys to work, and could probably walk to their

B

places of employment. There were always shops and pubs, churches and chapels, services and transport near by, easily reached on foot. Geographical proximity enabled a sense of community to be maintained, something that the twentieth-century 'estate' has somewhat neglected.

From 1870 onwards, visitors to London were astounded by the sheer size of the place. They were equally astonished by the large numbers of men always available to do odd jobs in the hope of earning a few pence. Casual labour, the uncertainty of a day's work, and the ever-glittering signs of the numerous pawn-brokers' shops testified to a class of poor for whom there could be little hope of betterment. In many cases, however, families did have cheap, rented accommodation near their work, and relaxation was had in the music halls, pubs, or parks. River trips were popular, while Epping Forest and Hampstead Heath provided large tracts of open space which could be enjoyed by all. Many honest, hard-working people, especially women, were grossly exploited, especially in the 'rag trade' where the sweat-shops flourished. The finery for the adornment of the richer classes was bought at the price of what amounted to slavery for those unfortunates who had to work in this trade. Often, prostitution was the only way out, while a woman who was fortunate enough to get a 'position' with a con-siderate family, even at a few pounds a year, regarded herself as being very lucky indeed. A dry bed, a warm house, free board, and the companionship of the household were all boons much appreciated when compared with the lot of those condemned to a short life of misery producing plumage for the wealthy.

The soup kitchens, mission halls, secondhand clothes shops, and cheap 'dining rooms' were all once familiar to the Victorian poor. The pawnbroker's, the gas-light, the pubs; the alchemy of bustle, degradation, squalor, poverty, death and disease; the magnificence of wealth and of State; the piety of Christians; the comradeship and the sheer mass of humanity; the humour and the sorrow; the hope and the despair were all part of the whole. It is not realistic to think of a candlelit ballroom in Belgravia without thinking of the flickering yellow gaslight in some stinking Whitechapel court at the same time. The odour of boiled cabbage and thin, unappetising soup that pervaded the stairs of tenements and back streets, undeniably mixed with other, even less savoury smells, was in con-trast to the groaning mahogany tables of the more fortunate houses, while the restaurants and clubs provided rich fare in enormous quantities.

The brothels of London and other great cities offered rich décor, food, drink, and entertainment. Men went to brothels not only to find something more agree-able than the arctic acquiescence of their spouses, many of whom were schooled in complete revulsion from their bodily functions, but to spend a relaxing hour or two with courtesans who were witty, uninhibited, naughty, perhaps vulgar but at any rate good fun. In such company, men could join in the latest songs, eat good food, swill champagne, and generally unwind. The cheapness of accommodation often enabled middle-class men, pillars of respectability and stern parents in the context of home or church, to keep a little mistress in Peckham or some other suburb. Perhaps the gay Cockney wenches who entertained so many bourgeois Londoners between the sheets of a large bed in a small villa or terrace house kept more than their lovers on an even keel. It is hard to imagine the stultifying atmosphere of so much that was respectable and middle-class doing other than destroying the fibre of a man. However, the Victorians were essentially realistic, and so long as the discretions were observed, all was well. Discovery meant dreadful things, as those *genre* painters who exhibited at the Academy pointed out so forcibly. To be morally suspect in the eyes of family or friends was a great burden. The visits to some *Pavillon d'Amour* was therefore carried out by cab, or by omnibus or train. Sometimes this could be hazardous, however, for even Dickens was caught in a train accident while actually travelling with his lady-friend. The domestic delights of a villa with a mistress installed within were considerably more attractive than the visit to the brothel for something other than food, drink, or gossip: the distemper known in earlier times as The Pox was rampant in Victorian days and the cure was non-existent.

The railways provided cheap, fast travel for many, and enabled even artisans to live in the newer suburbs, as the century progressed. The vast working-class and lower middle-class dormitories that spread during the last years of Victoria's reign were made possible by cheap travel by rail and tram. The hiss of steam and the scream of wheels on tram-lines became familiar to millions of people. The essence of Victorian cities was a variety and vitality. Unlike the great cities of the Renaissance and Classical times, Victorian cities gave forth an image of humanity and inhumanity in all their aspects: the bustling crowd and the sense of movement gave perhaps the strongest impression, whereas the public buildings were of secondary importance. There was no Cathedral, Parthenon, Abbey, Palace, Amphitheatre, or Civic Building to compare with the past in Victorian times. Victorian cities boasted railway stations, pubs, viaducts, tenements, town halls, museums, galleries, certainly, but the dominant mass of the Victorian city was the huge sprawl of houses for the people. Houses, flats, shops, pubs, and sheer mass of bricks and mortar lying between the main thoroughfares lined with shops and thronged with trams and cabs summed up a new phenomenon: the city of the common man.

Tennyson described 'streaming London's central roar' as long ago as 1852, and this roar was made by traffic, mostly horse-drawn, with the clank and screech of trains added to the cacophony. The streets, partly covered with square setts, but mostly, in residential areas, merely gravelled, and not properly surfaced, were hazards every Victorian pedestrian knew. Horse-droppings and mud played havoc with long dresses and shoes, and the crossing-sweeper was an essential attribute to any area of quality. The clearing of a path through the morass was a function of that lowly yet important figure who preceded any dignified persons wishing to preserve clean boots. The boot-scraper was therefore a feature no Victorian front-door could do without, and on its sharp ledge the worst thicknesses of mud or droppings could be removed. On very wet days many side streets became quag-mires, and there are legends of hapless servant-girls drowning in mud on their way back to their masters' houses late at night. Pavement shoe-shiners were as numerous as crossing-sweepers. A dry spell could alter the appearance of Victorian streets radically, not only in terms of mud, but, by drying the surface of the roads, making many shoe-shiners and crossing-sweepers temporarily redundant. At such times there would be a surplus of match-sellers, idlers, hailers of cabs, or odd-job men. Hardship and uncertainty went with colour and variety.

It must be remembered that by the end of the nineteenth century there were people then living who could remember the building of the docks, the railways, the bridges spanning the Thames, the tramways, the public buildings and monuments of which Trafalgar Square was perhaps the most outstanding example, and the great suburbs where the mass of Londoners lived. Similarly, there were parallels in almost every city and major town in the kingdom, although many villages and smaller towns had remained much as they had always been. The great hospitals, the market buildings, the theatres and music halls, and civic buildings added new monumental piles to the Victorian scene. The expansion of a school-building programme was equally striking, and, apart from the board schools, following acts for compulsory education, many schools and institutions were set up for adult education and for the more wealthy classes.

Had not the Victorian architects, engineers and politicians been aware of the practicalities and functions of city life, these enormous changes would hardly have occurred. Together with reforms and huge developments in public health, water supply, drainage, and the disposal of the dead, the unprecedented growth in population forced radical changes in the form and style of city living. Completely new structures had to be evolved, together with new methods of mass-production and comprehensive planning hitherto not experienced.

The purpose of this book is to attempt to show that Victorian buildings functioned as architecture. The choice of pictures was difficult, not because of a lack of material, but because, despite the destruction of so much fine Victorian work, there is such a vast amount left from which to make a selection.

I believe that, without a fundamental reappraisal of the achievements of the architects, engineers and builders active before the advent of the destroyers seduced us from our traditions, we will continue on the road to barbarism with terrifying results for our once-rich civilisation.

CHAPTER 2

New Materials and New Ideas

Simple was its noble architecture. Each ornament arrested, as it were, in its position seemed to have been placed there of necessity.

Voltaire, *Le Temple du Goût*

That unjustly maligned and cruelly misunderstood age when Victoria was Queen has been seen in many lights, most of them somewhat obscured by cloudy glass. The Victorians have been accused of practically every infamy in art and morals (witness the interest shown in Victorian perversions in recent times), but their achievements in realistic endeavour, brilliant daring in construction and uncompromisingly functional solutions to the problems of their day have tended to be underrated.

The revival of styles has been the subject of debate for over a hundred years, and the Victorians have been seen as romantics, as eclectics and even as plagiarists, but can the great mass of Victorian buildings ever be seen as mere copies of earlier prototypes? The Victorians, it is submitted, were original creators who made buildings and cities that were unmistakably of their own time.

Much has been made of the Gothic Revival in discussing the Victorians, but was there not a functional reason for the adoption of the pointed arch? As early as the 1770s, James Essex had said that the medieval architects were 'induced, or rather driven, to the use of the Pointed Arch by their practice of vaulting upon bows, and sometimes covering with such vaults spaces which were irregular; that is, not square, but longer in one dimension than another'.[1] Has not this aspect of the Gothic Revival been overlooked? The Gothic style, interpreted, had a functional advantage over classicism in that it was more adaptable to problems of roofing over irregular spaces, and it was more freely usable in the complex façades of the enormous public buildings of the nineteenth century than the rigid rules of classical styles would permit. Later developments of the Gothic Revival produced an architecture that was undoubtedly contemporary and could by no stretch of the imagination be regarded as a revival. It was a truly modern answer to the problems of the day.

Consider the work of Butterfield, for example. 'He delighted in that kind of ugliness—the ugliness of ruthless idealism and of the rejection of sentiment—that one finds . . . fifty years later, in early functional architecture.'[2] Furneaux Jordan describes him as a 'Gothic functionalist'.[3] Butterfield believed he was living in a revolutionary age, and that the Gothic should be transformed and reborn as an expression of that age. Old frescoes had not lasted, therefore use was made of the new industrially produced materials, such as glazed bricks, terra-cotta and Minton tiles. The interior of All Saints, Margaret Street, hard, rich and shiny with marble, tiles and glazed bricks, is an example of Butterfield's work as a functionalist in his ruthless use of modern materials and in his search for a true expression of his own time.[4]

There had been a functional tradition of good, straightforward design in the structures of the Industrial Revolution. This had been directly due to a continuing understanding of the value of craftsmanship, feeling for materials, even new materials, and to the existence of a living tradition in the simple decency of a vernacular architecture. Use had been made of cast-iron mass-produced products in factories, aqueducts, bridges, and churches, forerunning the theories of Butterfield. Many see the Crystal Palace as a turning-point, but the tradition and the prototypes were there, dating from the 1770s and reaching widespread acceptance in the Napoleonic Wars. The aqueducts on the Stratford canal are beautiful examples of cast-iron construction, with their standard railings, trough sections bolted together, and simple brick supports (plate 2). Early structures by Darby, Telford, Brunel and Stephenson had demonstrated the excellence of the material. Iron columns were recommended for practical reasons by Soane and others to help with the church-building programme after 1815. Nash used cast iron for his fake stone columns at Carlton House and in the Regent Street quadrant, and he made it utterly respectable by using it in the construction of Brighton Pavilion (1815-21). Thus the precedent was set for the use of cast iron on a lavish scale.

Conservatories were usually of conventional construction, with large windows, little more than the traditional orangery, in fact. Orangeries were constructed of brick or stone, and even of wood on occasion, and had slate or tile roofs. By the end of the eighteenth century glass roofs held in wooden frames were making their appearance. After the Napoleonic Wars, however, the development of the technology of cast iron, together with new methods of glass manufacture enabling sheets of glass some three times the maximum size of sheet available formerly, created entirely new possibilities in the field of conservatory design. Large, rot-free structures, curved and domed, became possible.

Glass-houses made of curved iron frames were suggested by G. S. Mackenzie in 1815, and followed up by T. A. Knight at Downton Castle in Shropshire.[5] Paxton's conservatory at Chatsworth (1837-40) was a tremendous step forward, and it was only a matter of time before the beautiful Kew Palm House, erected in 1844-8 by Richard Turner to designs by him and Decimus Burton, would show the elegant classes of the metropolis just how splendid the material could be. There was, however, a predecessor of the Kew Palm House that usually gets overlooked by commentators. In June 1839 the Marquis of Donegall laid the foundation stone of the Palm House in the Belfast Botanic Garden. The architect was (Sir) Charles Lanyon, the cast-iron frames were by Richard Turner of the Hammersmith Works at Ballsbridge, near Dublin, who was also the contractor, while the glazing was by Walker of Dublin. Turner appears in a Dublin Directory for the year 1813, and by 1836 he had moved to Ballsbridge. The two wings of the Belfast Palm House are the first known examples of the firm's work in Palm House design, and the Kew Palm House is to some extent derived from the experience gained in Belfast with Lanyon. Dr Eileen McCracken has carried out invaluable research into the origins and history of the Belfast Palm House, and her work was published in 1971 by the Ulster Architectural Heritage Society. Turner's work may have been evolved with his brother's help. Thomas Turner was an architect, and it is known that the brothers submitted a design for the Crystal Palace which was rejected. The genesis of the Kew Gardens design may be seen in Turner's creation in Belfast, while similar structures by the firm were erected at Portlaoise, Glasnevin, and Killikee.

The problem of the authorship of many pioneer designs using iron and glass has been the subject of much debate. Many of the design details were undoubtedly solved by the ironmasters themselves, and the names of celebrated architects, such as Burton and Lanyon, have tended to obscure the memory of the practical men who, in truth, provided the solutions. Paxton's Crystal Palace was clad in glass and timber, while Richard Turner specialised in structures of iron and glass only. The precise division of responsibility in the building of the Palm House at Kew has been adequately argued by scholars, and the rôle of Decimus Burton appears to have been, very properly, as architect, the designer of the form and style, while Turner's knowledge of detailing, prefabrication, and engineering enabled the elegant structure to be realised. Burton originally wanted a partly-wooden frame for his 'Winter Garden' to be erected in Regent's Park (now demolished), and it was Turner who produced a scheme based entirely on glass and iron. This 'Winter Garden' had many details in common with both Glasnevin and Belfast, and, subsequently, Kew. The worthy critic of *The Builder* observed of Turner's work that great praise was due for the manner in which it was carried out. Pertinently, it was observed that, as nearly 'all the work of this building' (Kew) had been 'accomplished by Irishmen', who were 'grateful for the employment it afforded them', it was hoped that the 'mechanics of that country' would be 'disposed to earn their bread in honesty and peace', as they were 'capable of executing works of that kind to the satisfaction of the professional gentlemen of this country'.

Turner's entry to the Great Exhibition Competition of 1850 was a remarkable design, based partly on his scheme for Lime Street Station roof at Liverpool, completed in the same year. Basically, the design showed a huge space nearly 2,000ft long and over 400ft wide, with transepts and a large glass dome over the crossing. The ends of the 'nave' as well as those of the transepts were to be closed with tracery of iron in the shape of a fan. This was Turner's work without the controlling hand of a great architect, and the result was something like a cross between a railway terminus and a cathedral, with a palm-house sitting on top. The scale, too, was enormous, and perhaps it is true to say that the proposal lacked the elegance and control of Paxton's work although it was undoubtedly a more practicable idea than the monstrous domed scheme produced by Brunel,

Wyatt, Jones, and Wild.

It was actually Charles Fox who calculated the design problems of the Crystal Palace, and it was he and his firm who made the working drawings. Aware of the measures necessary to ensure safety in a novel structure intended to receive millions of people attending the huge exhibition, and aware also of the lack of precedent for his work, Fox was determined to avoid any possibility of error. He worked eighteen hours each day for seven weeks, and as each drawing left his board, it was translated into ironwork by Henderson. As the calculations proceeded, so mock-ups were made, and empirical experiments were carried out to prove the strength of members. The design load was found to be more than adequate, and building was begun.

Perhaps one of the most fascinating aspects of the Crystal Palace, apart from the story of its building, is its ultra-simplicity. The stability of the joints between the columns and the beams was of paramount importance in a building where the methods tried in railway terminus construction did not apply. The Crystal Palace was a framed building, fully glazed, which took the glass-house concept one stage further, and indeed made future developments possible. It was, in truth, as Thackeray wrote:

> *A rare pavilion, such as man*
> *Saw never since mankind began,*
> *And built and glazed!*

Sir Joseph Paxton was in many ways the epitome of the Victorian functionalist. The man who was appointed Head Gardener to the sixth Duke of Devonshire in 1826 combined, with realism and piety, sound business sense and vision on a grand scale. As a collector and introducer of exotic plants, Paxton is of unprecedented importance in English horticultural history, his many-sided genius perhaps only challenged by that other remarkable gardener, John Claudius Loudon. Paxton's wall-conservatories, waterworks, Arboretum and Great Conservatory were extraordinary achievements. The Great Conservatory was the largest glass building in the world at the time of its building, and housed a marvellous collection of shrubs, trees and other plants. It was this building, more than any other, that gave Paxton the experience and knowledge which enabled him to translate his blotting-paper sketch for the Crystal Palace of 1851 into reality. Brunel's enormous domed structure of iron proposed as the result of a competition was superseded by Paxton's idea for a palace of iron and glass, and the Chatsworth Estate Office, working in conjunction with Chance Brothers and Fox Henderson & Co, realised Paxton's doodle, translating it into the vast structure in Hyde Park.[6] When we remember that the Crystal Palace was nearly 2,000ft long and 408ft wide, and contained over a quarter of a million panes of glass, some 4,500 tons of iron, and some 24 miles of guttering, and only took sixteen months to design and build, some idea of Victorian functional efficiency may be gauged.

Yet the story of system-building does not begin with the Crystal Palace, that marvellous structure that owes so much to Romanesque arcading and to Regency feeling for proportion. Although Paxton's system was later used by other designers, notably Owen Jones, mass-production of components probably began on something of a modern scale in the eighteenth century. It was at Abraham Darby's Bristol factory that an employee, John Thomas, perfected the casting of iron pots in sand. The success of this process enabled Darby to move to Coalbrookdale, and in 1778, by a logical extension of the casting methods, Abraham Darby III constructed a cast-iron bridge spanning the Severn Valley at what today is known as Ironbridge. This bridge was the forerunner of many other iron structures, and a system of industrialised construction comprising 'off the peg' parts was developed.

The functional advantages of prefabricated cast-iron components in architecture were quickly appreciated, and something more than mere structural consideration was given to the design of such parts.

The earliest cotton-mills of the eighteenth century were usually of four or five storeys, with walls of brick or stone, and timber floors. Generally speaking, these mills were quite narrow, owing to the structural limitations of wooden beams and floors. Naturally, the risks of destruction of the floors by fire or of weakening of the beams by rot or pests were very great. Between the years 1792 and 1793 William Strutt designed a new mill at Derby which incorporated fire-resistant construction. For the columns he used cast iron, already being produced in large quantities to support church galleries, to carry timber beams between which were brick arches spanning 9ft. The beams were protected by plaster, and the tops of the arches were covered with sand on which the brick floor-tiles were laid. A system of tie-rods was used to give additional support at the point where the columns and beams joined. Strutt's solution was rational, pragmatic, and utterly functional. Later developments by Bage at Shrewsbury (1796-7), Boulton and Watt at Salford (1799-1801), Bage at Leeds (1802-3) and Strutt at Belper (1803-4) used basically the same system substituting cast-iron beams for timber, so that a complete prefabricated system came into being, although in general, brick arches were used to support the floors and give fire-resistance.[7] The Salford mill was a very remarkable development, for the seating on the cast-iron beams heralds the flanged beam of later days, and it was the first centrally-heated mill. The hollow cast-iron columns served as circulation pipes for steam to provide heat, and there was gas-lighting throughout the factory.

It must be made clear, however, that the use of cast-iron components was not confined to industrial buildings. I have already mentioned the use of cast-iron columns in churches, and indeed splendid examples may be found in the Church of Ireland cathedral at Enniskillen, Co Fermanagh, and Rickman's Church of St George, Everton, has tracery of industrial patterns. One of the saddest losses of recent years was the delightful cast-iron-and-timber Renfield Street Church in Glasgow by James Brown of 1849, demolished in 1963. Gothick cast-iron tracing may also be found in St Alkmund, Shrewsbury, among other places, while cast-iron tombs occur in the vicinity of Coalbrookdale, fine specimens existing at Wellington and Madeley.

After the erection of the Crystal Palace in 1851, the respectability of cast iron as a building material was assured, and the product became fashionable, especially when used in conjunction with glass. Soon billiard-rooms, meeting-halls, kitchens, and all manner of spaces were being roofed with iron-and-glass structures. Those superbly functional products of the Victorian age, arcades, were developed, roofed in cast iron and glass, and they must be seen as the descendants of the Exhibition Hall known as the Crystal Palace. The charming Barton Arcade in Deansgate, Manchester, which is illustrated in plates 3, 4 and 5, shows how graceful such places could be. Cool in summer and protected in the winter, arcades were planned with shops on the ground floor, while often galleries on the upper levels would lead to offices. The detail, all mass-produced, is wonderfully put together in the Manchester example, and the whole is pleasing. The Barton Arcade was designed by Corbett, Raby and Sawyer in the early 1870s[8] using a 'Kit-of-Parts' cast at Macfarlane's Saracen Foundry in Glasgow.[9]

Goodhart-Rendel[10] draws our attention to the excellence of Victorian detailing, and to the good workmanship and design that made Victorian buildings infinitely more functional than much of our so-called 'functional' architecture in that they stood up to the rigours of smoky atmospheres much better and were strong enough and well enough designed to remain very presentable a century later. Of course this stemmed from the functional tradition of good straightforward design in the earlier period. The warehouses by the Thames, for example, are simple, functional answers to a problem, where materials are used in an utterly unaffected way (plate 6). As Steen Eiler Rasmussen puts it, the antique traditions were continued, and adjusted to the demands of a new age, while possibilities in new invention were utilised.[11] St Katherine's Docks, by Telford and Hardwick, must be seen as an example of this.

At the same time, the Victorians allowed the right of expression above pure function. There was a free relationship between inner and outer space, and between volumes, and a forceful use of artificial podia as urban elements in Victorian design. The sculptural unity of the environment and the new buildings was assured. Such a podium is found at St Pancras Station where it had the 'pure' functional purpose of raising the level of the terminus in order to secure good gradients and proper levels for the suburban stations, since the level of St Pancras is some 15ft above Euston Road. The space underneath was used as a cellarage for the Burton and other ale traffic.[12] The length of a beer barrel was adopted as the module for the spacing of the supports. Brick piers and arches would have occupied too much space, and so it was decided to use cast-iron columns, of which there are 720 at 14ft 8in centres, giving a floor of uniform strength throughout.[13]

It has been repeated *ad nauseam* that St Pancras Hotel by Scott and the train shed by W. H. Barlow (1812-1902) and R. M. Ordish (1824-86) coexist unhappily; that the junctions are bad, unresolved, and so on. One wonders if such critics have ever been to St Pancras and actually had a look at it. D. T. Timmins said of St Pancras Hotel in *The Railway Magazine* for June 1902 that it 'is an integral part of the station itself, and therefore cannot be treated of separately'. The details of the junctions between the shed and the brickwork are simply achieved (plate 7)—as simply as anything the early aqueduct-builders would have done—and the shed relates most beautifully to the great hotel. The shed is a long vault of Gothic arches, and spans a huge space within which trains, people, cabs and luggage could interrelate in the dry. Its girders join the Gothic brickwork in a satisfying rhythm, and the whole is a great piece of functional design, the elements of which are completely clear (plate 8).

The great roof of the train shed spans 240ft and is carried on arches, of which each side is a compound curve, springing from massive brick piers. The arches meet at an apex 105ft above the level of the tracks. The enormous structure was detailed by Ordish, and the complex scaffolding necessary for its erection was designed by J. G. N. Alleyne (1820-1912), the manager of the Butterley Company which fabricated the ironwork. The masonry and brickwork were constructed by Waring Brothers.[14] The shed was not the first, of course: it was the high spot of a superb series including King's Cross (1850) by Cubitt, and Paddington (1852) by Brunel and Digby Wyatt.

M. D. Wyatt wrote in 1851 that the use of iron would 'systematize a scale of form and proportion', and that engineering and architecture had drawn closer together towards a possible future 'consummation'. It was difficult, he wrote, to 'decide where civil engineering ends and architecture begins'.[15] New techniques and traditional methods were seen to come together as in the medieval cathedrals, for railway termini were seen as the cathedrals of the nineteenth century.[16]

Structure was expressed not only in the early buildings and engineering work of the century, but in mid-Victorian work too. Sheerness Naval Dockyard by G. T. Greene (1858) is a four-storeyed iron frame with bands of low windows and panels of corrugated iron. Yet, as Ruskin pointed out, 'the architect is not bound to exhibit structure; nor are we to complain of him for concealing it, any more than we should regret that the outer surfaces of the human frame conceal much of its anatomy; nevertheless, that building will generally be the noblest, which to an intelligent eye discovers the great secrets of its structure'. Ruskin said that gilding in architecture is no deceit because it is not understood for solid gold.[17]

The Victorians were hard-headed and ruthlessly functional in the design of railways, bridges, stations, sewers, pubs, warehouses and public-transport systems. The problems of metropolitan life grew with population, and the cholera epidemics of the 1830s and 1840s managed to get the reformers a hearing. Overcrowded graveyards were a source of scandal, and, together with the foul drinking-water and bad sewerage system, had been the targets of wrath for years. Discoveries in medicine after the cholera disasters made functional solutions to the problems absolutely necessary. In the 1830s the first great cemeteries were laid out and radicals advocated cremation;[18] in 1847 the eight boards of commissioners were amalgamated into one Metropolitan body for the drainage of London; and water supplies were subjected to scrutiny from 1821-40 in the *Reports and Evidence on Water Supply*. The fear of pestilence invaded the pages of the *Quarterly Review,* and in concerted attacks on bungling, incompetence and sheer apathy, it contributed to the setting up in 1855 of the Metropolitan Board of Works. The sewer and water-supply systems of London are perhaps as great monuments to the Victorian functionalists as any works, for public health was improved enormously by their efforts.[19]

In May 1863, one of the most spectacular pieces of Victorian functional design was commenced on site: Holborn Viaduct. Two lateral passages on either side supported the pavement, while the carriage-way was between them. The vaulted passages were divided into storeys. First was a space for cellars of the adjoining buildings; then against these was at the top a subway in which were laid the gas-, water- and telegraph-pipes; then a passage, and below these a vaulted chamber at the bottom of which was the sewer. An interesting design detail is the fact that the ventilation openings of the underground passages were in the pedestals of the lamp posts. A large tunnel and subway for pneumatic dispatch tubes were also incorporated[20] (fig 1 and plate 9). Holborn Viaduct was designed by William Haywood (1821-94), a pupil of George Aitchison. Haywood became assistant surveyor to the Commissioners of Sewers for London in 1845, and was chief engineer from 1846 until his death.[21] He worked closely with the celebrated Joseph Bazalgette. The architectural details of the Viaduct are handled supremely well, the granite columns and cast-iron arches with delicate decorations adding to the richness of London's fabric. The ironwork is coloured dark red, and discreetly gilded.

There had, in fact, been a prototype of the Viaduct projected by the architect,

F. Marrable. A drawing shows this 'Proposed High Level Road and Viaduct from St. Sepulchre's Church to Hatton Garden' (plate 10). Elegant shops were to be set in under the arches of the viaduct, while streets are indicated spanned by cast-iron bridges.

The overcrowding of the streets made it necessary to form a radically new method of transport, and so the Underground Railway was commenced in 1860. The success of the Metropolitan Railway created such an influx of bills for the proposed formation of railways that almost half of the City would have been demolished had the plans been implemented. A Committee of the two Houses was set up to examine the whole of the railway system and to rationalise the layout to maximum benefit. The admirable results formed the nucleus of a system which today is the core of the London Underground Railway. One only

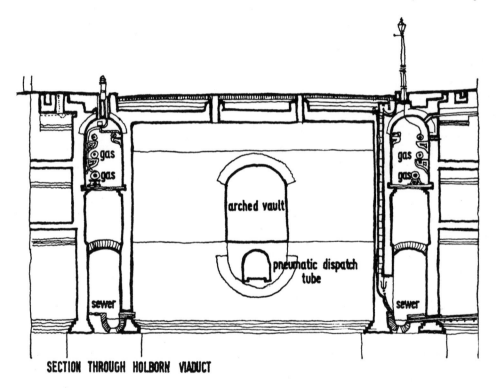

SECTION THROUGH HOLBORN VIADUCT

Fig 1   *Section through Holborn Viaduct (not to scale). Dating from 1863, Holborn Viaduct was designed by William Haywood. The two lateral passages support the pavements, while the main carriageway lies between. Cellarage for adjoining buildings was provided, and subways accommodated gas-, water- and telegraph-pipes, as well as a main sewer. Ventilation of the tunnels was through the pedestals of the lamp-posts. Drawn by James Stevens Curl*

has to travel on some of the older lines to be overwhelmed by the daring and simplicity of the Victorians' approach. The linking of all the termini, for example, by underground railway, connected so immediately with the main stations, is a marvellous feat. The immense brick-retaining walls, with their battered profiles and arched construction; the stations themselves, with liberal use of ironwork, valancing, tiles and glazed bricks; the tunnels of brick and metal; and the magnificent clarity of it all, show the Victorians to us as functionalists of an extraordinary degree of integrity. The result is a great architectural expression, as powerful as a Roman aqueduct, and as much a part of that great tradition which was handed down from Regency days.

The early Victorian schemes for urban viaducts have a grandeur of their own. The interesting proposals for the London Grand Junction Railway published by G. S. Tregear (plate 11) show a railway carried on arches forming a viaduct from the low-lying ground at Skinner Street, Clerkenwell, to the heights of Camden Town. The reason for the viaduct was two-fold: to enable the railway to function, since the gradient would have been too steep if the tracks had been laid on the ground; and to raise the railway over the streets to avoid interference with traffic and pedestrians. The monumental flight of steps leading to a simple gate should be noted.

Consider the Victorian pub. The materials, like those in the railways, are ideal for the job: tiles, zinc, marble, mahogany, copper, good glass and glazed bricks contrast with the pseudo-genteel bars of today which offer laminated plastics, carpets, and fabric-covered chairs which are hopelessly dirty and indescribably tatty in a very short time. In pub design the Victorians win hands down, since their materials were hard, durable, cleanable and looked well. Pubs are for drinkers and for sociability. The Victorians made the pubs pleasant places to be in by using rich, strong, bold, durable materials in equally strong designs, so that the pubs lasted, despite the drunks. Victorian pub design, in short, was functional, and will be analysed in Chapter 6.

Another aspect of Victorian functionalism, of course, was that of expressing an idea. Commercial stability was epitomised in the great classical banks by Cockerell; piety was suggested by the modern austere Gothic of Blomfield, Street and Butterfield; while civic pride, especially in a newly rich and growing manufacturing centre, is symbolised by the extraordinary Town Hall at Manchester, by Alfred Waterhouse. Goodhart-Rendel said of this building that 'its nobly architecturalised construction, the mingled grandeur and convenience of its planning, the magnificent massing of its composition, and the complete harmony of every decorative element in it with every other, have still to be surpassed'.[22] Waterhouse's 'Gothic' Town Hall (1868-77) could only be Victorian, and it could only have been built in a northern manufacturing town (plate 13).

It filled a void, a need, and it functioned as a symbol and as a centre for newly acquired civic pomp. It must therefore be seen as a functional building.

The Victorian age still permitted the marriage of technique and creative imagination. The result was an architectural expression of strength, daring, boldness, power, and functional greatness. A rupture has occurred since then, with the decline in craftsmanship; with the increase in the compartmentation of disciplines and activities, and therefore the widening of the gulf between the 'professional' and the man who actually builds the job; and with the over-emphasis on the purely measurable criteria from which the imagination and real feeling for materials and design must be excluded.

The Victorians have lessons for us in many things, not least of which is their contribution to the functioning of cities and buildings, and other works that form the physical structure of the city and contribute by their reality to the spiritual qualities of that city. They were successful in creating an architecture which could delight the eye. Would that our own 'functionalists' did the same. Instead we have buildings which are really rather tired-looking after only short lives, and which are usually subject to enormous problems such as solar heat gain, to name but one aspect where the excuse of 'functionalism' proves grotesquely illusory.

Today, we are busy destroying the fabric which the Victorians created, believing them to have been something other than the realists they were. Our replacements show our age to be the real age of eclectics, of non-functionalists, and of the real philistines.

Notes to this chapter are on pages 115-16

C

CHAPTER 3

Symbols, Cathedrals and Churches

When I lately stood with a friend before [Amiens Cathedral] he asked me how it happens that we can no longer build such piles. I replied: Dear Alphonse, men in those days had convictions (*Überzeugungen*). We moderns have opinions (*Meinungen*). It requires something more than an opinion to build a Gothic Cathedral.

Heinrich Heine, *Confidential Letters to August Lewald on the French Stage*, no 9

Heine, of course, was quite right. Expertise, empirical experiment, sensibility, style, craftsmanship and devotion all contributed to the Gothic cathedrals. What Heine was getting at was the fact that those buildings famed throughout the world for their qualities, and which arouse an agreeable response in us, are based on aesthetic values owing their origins to a mystic union of man and the universe. The religious aspects of creative work were once clear, and the belief in order was reflected in the creative act and in its products. Purpose was given to creation by a fundamental belief in the wholeness of the world and its place within a totality itself the product of a Creator.

Today, we are sundered from the eternal verities by an ever-growing mountain of statistics, data, empirical material and so-called 'measurable' values. The picture is one of meaningless chaos, being ever redirected by the latest pronouncements of the fashionable pundits and arbiters of taste.

The Greek temple of the Doric period has been the subject of much debate. The mind unversed in metaphysics will seek to explain that Doric architecture was evolved because of economic and technical advances which made it possible to reinterpret an architecture of timber in stone. Such a view only attempts to show how Doric architecture came about, but it signally fails. Why bother to expend so much energy and time on problems of entasis, proportion, fluting, and decoration, if all that is being accomplished is the reinterpretation of a petrified tree? A Doric column, whatever the reasons for its manufacture, is the visible symbol of the creative power of a cultured people. The temple thus became a symbol of the mystery of the eternal present, and reconciled the earth-bound spirit of the Greeks to the harmony of the cosmos. The care lavished on detail and proportion was the linking element that fused the parts in an ordered entity.[1]

The surge of ecclesiastical building activity in Europe during the Middle Ages gave one chronicler the impression that the world was 'clothing itself everywhere in the white robe of the Church'.[2] The Gothic cathedrals built from the mid-twelfth to the fifteenth century are outstanding examples of that activity. The medieval cathedrals were unique expressions of the religious concern of the period. They were the 'best that architecture had to tell, for [they] typified the aspirations of man at the moment when man's aspirations were highest'.[3]

The difference between the Doric temple and the Gothic cathedral is only one of emphasis. The former is static and earth-bound, whilst the latter aspires ever upwards to the heavens. The medieval cathedral was a symbol of man's place within the universal scheme of things: it was the product of co-operative effort over a long period; it told the stories of universal religion in visual and readily understood terms; and it in itself became the expression of paradise on earth. Its design was based on metaphysical and symbolic ideas of measurement from Biblical and Platonic sources.[4] Indeed, Plato's *Timaeus* discussed the laws of mathematical relationships, and these laws contained the basis for much of the geometrical origins of *mandala* symbols, especially the cube. The significance of numbers and their magical properties was propounded by Pythagoras when he founded the government at Croton, and even today there are survivals of the Pythagorean culture, one of which is the habit in Calabria of spitting three times in the presence of a child being suckled, and the shouting, also three times, of 'otto-nove'.[5]

The *mandala*, as explained by Jung, von Franz and others,[6] is a symbol of the totality of the psyche in all its aspects, including the relationship between man, the universe and nature. This relationship has been graphically represented by many cultures, and expressed as circles, polygons, labyrinths, cubes, squares and other figures which are regular and which, if divided, can be seen to have a centre. The circle and the polygon, for example, can be subdivided radially so that a design like a compass results. The thousand-petalled lotus of Brahma is a *mandala*, and Brahma is seen, turning his eyes to the cardinal points of the compass, and this stance is known as 'primary orientation'. To the Zen Buddhist, the circle represents order, enlightenment, and perfection, and the circle divided radially into eight represents the entire cosmos in its relationship to divine powers. This figure is found in ideal-city plans, such as Palma Nova (which was the Venetian fortress town and one of the few *mandala*-planned cities to be built), Utopian town planning schemes of the Renaissance and Baroque periods, and even in Ebenezer Howard's diagrams for his Garden City.[7] The *mandala* is the awakener and preserver of life. The way in which it is combined with other figures, however, may give prominence to one meaning or another. As Giedion points out, the 'total significance of circular forms cannot be confined within the bounds of exact definition'.[8]

The Renaissance masters merged all consciousness with a new ordered coherence of pattern based on *mandala* forms, but these were already familiar from time immemorial. The crude circles and squares, the pyramids with square bases, the labyrinths of ancient minds, were all *mandala*s, and expressions of man's awareness of his place in relation to a cosmic force of creation. The Greek key motif was a stylised version of the labyrinth. Stonehenge was a *mandala*, as was Avebury.

The medieval cathedral, with its carefully planned orientation, abounded in *mandala* symbols. The rose window, ablaze with coloured glass, is an obvious example, but less obvious is the fact that the cathedral was a *mandala* itself. It was a visible reflection, a symbol of the invisible world, of paradise, and it must be remembered that, to the medieval mind, the symbol was real, and not merely an allegory. Life was a pilgrimage to the ultimate goal. The pilgrimages to the cathedrals were symbols of life's journey. That journey ended in the paradise of the cathedrals where, bathed in the light of thousands of candles that flickered in the mellow and mysterious vastness, the human spirit was uplifted by the ancient liturgy. The senses were delighted by visual pleasures; by the smell of incense, burning candles and oil; and by the splendid sound of plainsong and complex polyphony.

The use of light was highly significant. The stained-glass windows not only told the stories of Christianity in richly patterned and coloured masterworks, but represented the mean between the physical and the metaphysical. The patterns of tracery were themselves the microcosms of the patterns used throughout the cathedrals themselves. The geometrical figures known from ancient times were, as we have seen, of great significance as symbols and as *mandala* forms. The *Vesica Piscis,* two inter-connected circles; the square; the circle; the golden section; the equilateral triangle (which, of course, fits within a circle or polygon, and is therefore a *mandala*); and the labyrinth all were found in the cathedrals. The labyrinth, for example, was represented in the leadwork of the stained glass, and in the patterns in the floors of the cathedrals. These labyrinths were also symbols of life's pilgrimage, with many tortuous ways, until the goal was reached. The cathedral was itself a labyrinth of chapels, columns, and devotional altars, which the pilgrim had to visit and find his way through before he had completed the pilgrimage. The labyrinth was a symbol of the Holy Grail, not only the cup from which Christ drank, but the object of desire which led the pilgrim through life to paradise.

The *Vesica Piscis,* a *mandala* which embraces two overlapping circles, is of profound significance in the symbolism of Gothic architecture. It is the very basis of the pointed arch! It is the eye of the needle through which the rich man cannot pass, and it has many geometrical variants which may also be found in the cathedrals. Each circle will contain equilateral triangles, but so will the two Gothic arches found by the intersection (fig 2). In addition, the figure possesses so many geometrical properties of subdivision, multiplication, overlaying, and embracing of other figures that it is hardly surprising to find it used so often as the basic motif of so many design treatments in the Middle Ages.[9] Obviously, the all-embracing significance of such a figure, not only in metaphysical but in geometrical terms, made it ideal as a basis for construction, and got over the cumbersome problems of vaulting with circular arches. The functional versatility of the pointed arch was ideal for the complexities of a great medieval cathedral. It is small wonder that the figure of Christ is often found sculpted within a *Vesica Piscis* above the portal of great churches.

Paradise and the ordinary world were close in the individual mind. The town clustered round the church or cathedral, where all that human artistic endeavour could create was lavished. The profane and the sacred were near each other, embraced by a sense of order and continuity. Today, we are all specialists, bogged down in detail and trivia, and divorced from a cosmic experience by the compartmentalisation of modern life. We have lost the meaning of the totality because of attention to purely measurable things. The architectural profession of today is more concerned with cost control, systems, and other matters far removed from the verities with which architecture is concerned. The universe is still mysterious, and yet we have forgotten the mysteries: we are so mesmerised by physics that we have lost the language of metaphysics.

All this may appear to be a digression. It is not. It is entirely relevant to a study of the Victorians considered as functionalists. Architecture is related to the

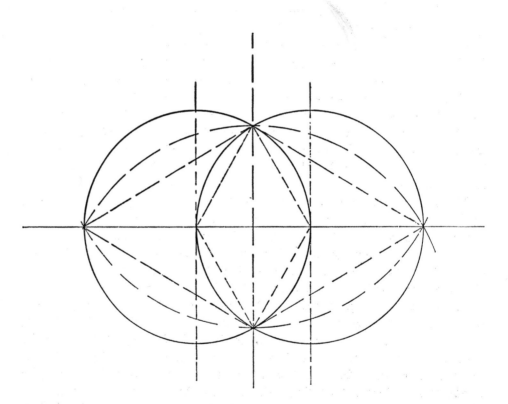

Fig 2   *The* Vesica Piscis. *Note the equilateral triangles and the Gothic arches formed by the relationships between the two mandala forms. The all-embracing significance of such a figure, not only in terms of metaphysics, but of geometry, made it ideal as a basis for construction, and got over the problems of vaulting spaces not square on plan. The functional versatility of the pointed arch was ideal for the complexities of a great medieval cathedral as well as those of a Victorian office-block. Drawn by James Stevens Curl*

phenomenal world of visual experience, and therefore to aesthetics, and not just to physics or costs. Our response to a medieval environment is not only that of an historian or an archaeologist, for it has something of an awareness of high aspirations to spiritual things. The disenchantment with contemporary design, and indeed the environmental crisis (which some say is coming, but which is patently with us now), may be traced back to the fact that designers no longer know anything about the ancient classical figures that are not merely systems for proportioning buildings, but which have their roots in the subconscious mind of man. The alienation of modern art and architecture, their boredom and their rejection by the mass of society are explainable. Modern expression is not based on those *mandala* forms which are the symbols of man's deep inner need to be related to the world in which he lives. For the first time in the history of the world, those eternal symbols are missing from what we create, and so mankind can no longer respond to the art and architecture of his period. He cannot, because his nature cannot recognise anything any more. It is interesting that popular arts, in the form of poems and prints, rely on traditional symbolic or representational patterns, and 'pop-music' retains the simple harmonics and chords familiar from late medieval times. Modern 'serious' music has become incomprehensible to most people, and it is so esoteric and divorced from tradition that it no longer can play any real part in the culture of the community.

The traditional symbols are homeless in the realities of the modern commercial world, and architecture has become a stranger to the symbol. In the Middle Ages, Europe dwelt, worshipped and worked in an environment created in the image of an authentic spiritual vision. If we wish to learn anything of the triumph of the spirit, we must relearn the lost language of the symbols as found in the medieval cathedrals and earnestly recorded by the Victorians. We must regain our equilibrium in the cosmos, and we can only do this by truly creative acts. We cannot create until we understand the language of creation. We can be retaught that lost tongue by a study of the systems of proportion, of symbolism and of expression found in the buildings of the past.

We are fortunate in having so many Victorian buildings which offer us an alphabet as a key to what Nietzsche called 'this language of the universal'. As Eastlake remarked of the Gothic Revival: '[the] renewal in this country, of a taste for Medieval architecture, and the reapplication of those principles which regulate its design, represent one of the most interesting and remarkable phases in the history of art'.[10] But he went on to observe that, unlike the Renaissance in Italy,[11] which was associated with a revival in the study of classic literature, the Gothic Revival 'fails to exhibit, even in its earliest development, many of those external causes to which we are accustomed to attribute a revolution in public taste'.[12] Clark showed, however, that there were indeed literary precedents for the

Gothic Revival, from Shakespeare to Horace Walpole, and from Gray to Pugin, not to mention the liturgical requirements of the Tractarians and the Cambridge Camden Society.[13]

The Victorians rediscovered the Middle Ages, and, taking their cue from the north European cities of the Hanse, often built their Gothic buildings in brick. Butterfield was especially influenced by the brick architecture of Lübeck and the Baltic ports. It was but a short step from this to the use of brick for even 'French Gothic of the thirteenth century', a popular style with James Brooks, John F. Bentley, G. E. Street and others. The use of hard glazed tiles has already been mentioned in connection with Butterfield, but again, there were medieval precedents. The rediscovery of medieval patterns for floor and wall tiles rescued a host of fine designs from oblivion, while the renewed art of stained-glass manufacture and design was responsible for some great Victorian masterpieces. There can be few examples more successful than that great eastern rose at Waltham Abbey, by Burne-Jones, set in a splendid Gothic window by Burges, all the more daring for being in an otherwise Romanesque nave! The work of Clayton and Bell, Kempe and others brings richness and mystery to many Gothic churches, and often restores something lost to real medieval buildings.

Victorian craftsmanship in stone and metalwork enriched architecture, and often works of considerable originality resulted, produced by designers such as Pearson, Street, Burges, Butterfield and Bentley.

The extraordinary fact about Victorian Gothic was that many sensitive men knew there was something there that was worthwhile and important, and although Pugin had given a specious explanation in *Contrasts*, when he insisted that Gothic was the only 'Christian' (ie Roman Catholic) architecture, there was undoubtedly a tremendous feeling that Gothic had something which was valuable.[14]

Imagine the young architect of the 1830s and 1840s who saw only a mass of buildings of sub-Italianate stucco going up, and who saw no opportunity other than to design buildings on classical lines. Imagine the constrictions of symmetry, classical Orders and decoration. It had all been done before. He could no longer build in stone, as the expense was generally prohibitive except in Scotland and in the North, and so stucco was the order of the day. Even the remarkable genius of Sir John Soane, which had a tremendous influence on architecture and architects for a short period, was steeped in classical tradition. Imagine the liberating breath that Gothic brought to architecture. Asymmetry, coloured brickwork, and a new freedom in the invention of naturalistic decoration were only a few of the boons that came with it. The enthusiasm with which Gothic was greeted was partly due to relief at finding new possibilities, partly due to mistaken notions as to its 'Christian' or 'moral' value, but also due to a response in the young to the great array of geometrical variations presented by the 'style', an array which owed its richness to ancient symbols known from the earliest of times.

The devotional aspects of Victorian Gothic architecture were balanced by a rediscovery of the wealth of decoration for walls, roofs, capitals, glass, altars, floors, and fittings. The symbol glossary was used to great effect, and the rediscovery of the medieval architectural and sculptural catalogue helped in the production of Victorian churches which, although undeniably Victorian, have the authentic medieval atmosphere. Something of the harmony of the divine may be found in great churches of the Victorian period, for example All Saints', Margaret Street, by Butterfield; St Peter's, Vauxhall, by J. L. Pearson; and the East London churches by James Brooks. In all these cases, however, bricks are used for the interiors, quite unlike the true medieval churches in the styles supposedly resurrected. A Brooks church is always recognisable as by Brooks, and Butterfield's personal preferences make his buildings equally memorable. The inventiveness and success of these Victorian architects are due to their understanding of planning, massing, detail, colour and the language of medieval figurations or symbols that could be combined in an infinite number of ways. The straight Germanic façade of Butterfield's church of St Augustine, Queen's Gate, is more than an interpretation of the medieval churches of Brandenburg or Pomerania. All Saints', Margaret Street, is more than a revival: it is a glowing and noble original work filled with the spirit of creativity based on the language of ancient symbols.

It certainly requires more than an opinion to build a Gothic Cathedral, or a great Victorian Gothic church, for that matter. It is not surprising that when Pugin had become accepted after the publication of *Contrasts,* he was inundated with commissions, and in *The True Principles of Pointed Christian Architecture* he dealt with the practicalities of building in Gothic. As Alexandra Gordon Clark says, it was 'as a practising architect—Pugin the functionalist—that he spoke'.[15] Pugin himself said that 'there should be no features about a building which are not necessary for convenience, construction, or propriety; second, that all ornament should consist of enrichment of the essential construction of the building'. Furthermore, the 'external and internal appearance of an edifice should be illustrative of, and in accordance with, the purpose for which it is destined'. Only in the Gothic style could buildings be functional, appropriate, and true, for even an old English parish church as originally used, 'was one of the most beautiful and appropriate buildings that the mind of man could conceive; every portion of it answered both a useful and a mystical purpose'. Precisely so, and although the full meaning of ancient symbols may have escaped Pugin, he clearly understood something of the significance of medieval architecture beyond his 'moral' concepts which were probably only a reaction against his times, not the embodiment of a sincere intellectual creed.

Pugin, despite his obvious faults as a theoretician, believed in rational construction as the basis of good architecture. In his *An Apology for the Revival of Christian Architecture in England* (1843) he wrote that he was not seeking to 'produce mere servile imitators of former excellence of any kind, but men imbued with the consistent spirit of ancient architects, who would work on their principles, and carry them out as the old men would have done, had they been placed in similar circumstances and with similar wants to ourselves'. In short, Pugin saw a time coming when the principles of 'natural building' would be relearnt in a renewed Christian society, so that something of the true spirit of medieval times could be recaptured. Unfortunately, the growing specialisation of crafts and professions, together with the further divorce of craftsmen from acts of spontaneous creation due to the Victorian architectural practice of detailing everything, put his vision into a limbo which population growth, industrialised components, and false architectural theories have made more black and deep.

Pugin himself wrote of his ideal church:

[the] towers served a double purpose, for in them hung the solemn sounding bells to summon the people to the offices of the church, and by their lofty elevation they served as bearers to direct their footsteps to the sacred spot. Then the southern porch, destined for the performance of many rites—the spacious nave and aisles for the faithful—the oaken canopy carved with images of the heavenly Host ... the fretted screen and rood loft—the mystical separation between the sacrifice and the people, with the emblem of redemption carried on high and surrounded with glory—and the great altar, rich in hangings, placed far from irreverent gaze, and with the brilliant eastern window terminating the long perspective; while the chantry and guild chapels, pious foundations of families and confraternities, contributed greatly to increase the solemnity of the glorious pile.

In Pugin's own completed work, the symbol is realised, and the picturesque image becomes a functional reality.

Notes to this chapter are on pages 116-17

CHAPTER 4

An Inventive Architect, or, Acrobatic Gothic, Freely Treated

Men who love buildings are their own undoers,
and need no other enemies.

Marcus Crassus, quoted by Plutarch
in *The Life of Marcus Crassus*

Many architects derived their professional ancestry from Pugin and others. Butterfield set about the task of building Gothic structures using modern materials. Some claimed that Gothic was an indigenous style, and of the people, but it was clear that 'the people' were indifferent: for the Revival owed everything to the cultivated, literate class. Opinion could appeal to what Halsey Ricardo called 'The High Court of Antiquarian Research'[1] for acceptance or damnation of a building. Indeed, the Ecclesiologists wielded great power, and could wreck an architect's reputation overnight. Butterfield escaped such strictures partly through this enormous knowledge of medieval architecture, and partly through his realism in building for his own time on strictly functional lines. Others were not so lucky.

The problem was that many of the more pedantic followers of Ecclesiology tried to fit their theories of symbol, convention, historicism, and creativity into a preconceived notion of moral worth and beauty. This is why there was a change from Early English to Decorated, and then to French Gothic of the thirteenth century, each phase of each style acclaimed to be the only 'true' one. Theorists attacked one another with venom, and Ruskin was among the most poisonous. In one case, the victim of pedantry attempted to fight back, and his fate was interesting. Enoch[2] Bassett Keeling is one of those names sure to excite the contempt of Ecclesiologists and students of the mainstream of academically correct Gothic Revival. His strange and wilful architecture, however, was remarkably distinctive, and *The Builder* noted the 'originality and effectiveness' of his work.[3]

Bassett Keeling, born in Sunderland in 1837, began his training as an articled pupil of Christopher Leefe Dresser, of Leeds, becoming headmaster of a local school of art there, and set up his own practice in London in December 1857. His most notorious building was the Strand Music Hall, erected on the site of the western part of Aldwych as it cuts northwards from the Strand. This ambitious and lavish hall had 'commodious and elegant dining and smoking rooms', bars and buffets, as well as the huge hall itself. The building was advanced for its time, provision for escape being ample, and the lighting being through the ceiling, a system devised by the architect. This ceiling was composed of coloured glass in the panels, and prisms set in the soffites of the hollow ribs, with baskets of lanterns formed by prisms set at the intersections. The ribs of the ceiling were fitted with moulded zinc sash frames to hold the sheets of coloured glass laid loose on indiarubber for ease of cleaning and avoidance of vibration or breakage. There was a total absence of gas fittings in the hall, with the exception of the footlights. The space between the ceiling and roof formed a lighting chamber, and the structure was of wrought iron and zinc, carried on brick walls and cast-iron columns and brackets.

There were over 1,000 prisms of pure glass, 15in long and 3in wide, set alternately in the ribs with strips of plate glass, ground on one side, and having stars cut upon them. The lantern pendants at the rib intersections were formed of prisms of pure crystal, the light, in small jets of gas, being brought down into them below the level of the ceiling proper which was lighted from above. The products of combustion and the foul air were drawn out together, the lighting was very rich, and deleterious effects on decorations were avoided.[4]

The cast-iron columns had wrought-iron copper foliate caps, and the deep brackets and balcony fronts were also of cast iron. The total impact of the interior was intricate, rich, and startling. The raked balconies, heavily enriched, the tall cast-iron columns, the huge cast-iron brackets supporting the enormous cornice, and the glittering ceiling were combined in a veritable Aladdin's cave of entertainment architecture (plate 14).

The Strand Music Hall was inaugurated in 1864, and a pamphlet—*The Strand Musick Hall: Historye of ye Building*—contained an apologia for its 'eclectic continental gothic'. The venture was not a success, and the Hall was a 'failure from the day of its opening'.[5] This was partly due to the architecture, which suggested to John Hollingshead a 'decorator's studio, overloaded with samples picked from all nations'.[6] When Sir Richard Burton saw it, he considered his education completed, never having seen 'under one roof, anything like this remarkable building'.[7] It exhibited, according to *The Builder*,[8] 'many eccentricities of design'; nevertheless, 'it had the merit of originality and effectiveness, and it was not only at the time something novel in its way, but had even some influence on the style of other buildings erected soon after it; and it is not every architect who could say that of one of his works'.

The Strand Music Hall gave Bassett Keeling his first controversial publicity on a national scale, but it was also responsible for the first of the disasters that were to overtake him. Although an architect, H. H. Collins, worked on the building with Keeling, the design is undoubtedly by Keeling, and exhibits all the angular spikiness so characteristic of his early work (plate 16). Keeling seems to have been singularly unfortunate in his choice of business associates, and it is a matter of speculation how far Collins was involved in the subsequent crash. The venture was in trouble in 1865, for *The Times*[9] reported an action by one Drew before the Court of Common Pleas to recover £300 for the erection of mahogany counters and plate glass. The jury found for the plaintiff, but there appears to have been no money available, for an official liquidator was appointed in February 1865.[10] In the same month, under a Notice and First Meeting of Creditors, *The Times* reported the name of Enoch Bassett Keeling, of Verulam Buildings, Gray's Inn, and Napier Terrace, Islington, Architect. Keeling's debts were given as £3,021, inclusive of liabilities upon shares, and he attributed his difficulties to losses in connection with the Music Hall.[11] During 1864-5, Keeling was in partnership with one Tyrie, probably a James Edward Tyrie, who was a stockjobber in the City, and who also went bankrupt in 1865. It is clear from the original drawings of various churches that Keeling was solely responsible for the architecture. Tyrie must have been some kind of financial partner, and may himself have been involved in the Strand Music Hall project. The partnership was, however, dissolved in 1865, and Keeling continued in practice from 1 Verulam Buldings. The problem was more than failure in financial terms, for a large part of the criticism of the Strand Music Hall came from the Ruskinites. Keeling had committed the unforgivable 'sin' of applying the 'moral' style of Ruskin and Street to a vulgar music hall! He was violently attacked, and defended himself, pointing out that he 'may have been eccentric', but that no one could accuse him of plagiarism. Indeed, he claimed to have produced an 'eclectic design, but it is eclecticism and not patchwork'. 'What I have wished to secure,' he declared, 'is general picturesqueness, and in detail piquancy and crispness.'

A letter in *The Building News* of 25 November 1964 was thoroughly condemnatory of the Strand Music Hall. 'Mr Bassett Keeling', wrote 'J.C.', 'deserves the hearty thanks of the architectural profession for having at last furnished a subject on which its most opposite factions are agreed in a unanimous verdict. Gothic, or Classic, conservative or progressive, all join to condemn the Strand Music Hall.' The sentence may be in the main a just one; but some of the reasons given for it are highly amusing.

'J.C.' went on to compare the approaches of two correspondents who clothed their buildings with either an Italian or a medieval dress. 'Mr Keeling's theory of art appears to be the exact opposite' of the 'copiers', for his 'aim would be to copy nothing—and the title "Eclectic" scarcely applies to his work'. The past, according to 'J.C.', was discarded altogether by Keeling, and although many of the features of the Music Hall were 'suggestive', scarcely any would bear examination, and some were 'positively repulsive'. 'The Strand Music Hall, with all its failings, contains ample evidence of work on the part of its designer, and shows a vitality not to be traced in the copies of "our village churches" or the "Reform Club", which the sleepy school of architects are so fond of giving us.' Other correspondents accused Keeling of 'vulgarity', 'lack of originality', and 'want of poetic and national taste'. However, we might consider that 'vulgarity' might be an excellent attribute of a Music Hall.

An article in *The Building News* for 21 October 1864 perhaps describes Keeling's style most accurately, for the title of the article is 'Acrobatic Gothic'. The 'undoubtedly talented' architect had expressed the purpose of the building in his architectural work. The Hall was a fit setting for the highest 'jinks and most comic capers' and these would not fail to be in harmony with the 'high jinks' played in stone, brick, and iron upon the façades by Bassett Keeling. However, the author of the article continued, if 'such enduring materials are not the proper vehicles

D

for jocular experiments, and the ordinary frequenters of the adjoining streets are not fitting butts to be poked fun at continually; if it be reprehensible to play the fool with the recognised styles of architecture, and to parody its best features, then grave censure cannot be witheld from the author of the eccentricities which are displayed in every part of this building.' Furthermore, that 'Gothic architecture should have been the type chosen' for the Strand Music Hall 'was unfortunate indeed for the Gothic style.' Eccentricity of proportion, puerilities in the detail, and excess tendency towards squatness and stumpiness were further faults heaped upon the pile of anti-Keeling criticism. It was hoped that Keeling's next essay would be 'more temperate and better studied', and that his 'genius for practical joking may be exercised upon other work than architecture'.

H. H. Collins, who assisted Keeling in the supervision of the building, denied any connection with the actual design in a letter to *The Building News* of 21 October 1864, although he bore testimony to the 'almost Herculean labour' Keeling expended on the work. According to Collins, however, Keeling had been 'bold in the practice of mistaken rules'.

Keeling wrote an hilarious letter which was published on 28 October under the heading 'Acrobatic Criticism *v.* Acrobatic Gothic—The Strand Music Hall', in which he lampooned the critics with a pen suitably dipped in gall. By November, however, the anti-Keeling faction was becoming vicious. 'The carpenter's Gothic decoration over the stage is truly AWFUL!' wrote one correspondent in *The Building News* of 4 November 1864. Another letter claimed that it was 'the coarse hugeness of everything which offends', and then wallowed in xenophobia, denouncing all continental Gothic in favour of the home-brewed variety.

The battle of the styles was joined. 'A Classic Man' wrote that the 'Gothic men seem to have been aroused at last to a sense of the dignity and interests of their own peculiar style, and utterly and completely repudiate Mr. Bassett Keeling's latest production . . . Now, Sir, it appears to me very much like the pot calling the kettle black. One of the chief objects in designing a building is to make it tell its own tale, or, in other words, to look like what it is intended for. Now Mr. Keeling's building does look like a Music Hall—it does not look like a church—which is more than can be said of nine out of ten Gothic buildings destined for secular purposes. In the building itself we may suppose that spirits and liquors of all kinds will be freely indulged in, and will perhaps yield the largest profits to the share-holders. The pipe and cigar will be puffed to their fullest extent; and the nature of the entertainment will be a jumble of serious and comic songs, of bits from favourite operas and burlesques on them, of all kinds of acrobatic performances, tight-rope, trapeze, &c . . . Now the interior and exterior of the building in their decoration are a very fair index or type of its future destination. The profusion of vine and other leaves symbolises the mixtures of liquors and spirits; the notches and chamfers will, like the nicotean weed, end, we hope with Mr. Burges, in smoke; and the jumble of serious and curious busts, the gilt statues inside, and all the other ornamental features, impersonate the entertainment given, and the people who listen to it.'

But Keeling himself exposed the stupidities of his critics, one of whom he suggested, if commissioned to cut a man's throat would use an oyster-shell, and the other would use a razor. 'Classic Man', he said, however classic he may have been with a pencil, was a 'very Goth' with his pen. The 'poor unfortunate edifice', he wrote of the Strand Music Hall, 'is arraigned before a self-constituted professional tribunal, and charged as a building, but still, being a music-hall—

1. That it is Gothic.
2. That it is not Classic.
3. That it is neither.
4. That it has tried to be Gothic, and is not.
5. That it is a practical joke.
6. That it is a serious mistake.
7. That it exactly expresses its purpose.
8. That it does nothing of the kind.
9. That being a music-hall it does not bear comparison with the following buildings:—Mr. Woodward's insurance office in Bridge-street, Blackfriars; the half-timbered and weather-tiled houses of Sussex and Kent; St. Paul's Cathedral; Mr. Webb's shops in Worship-street; Sir C. Barry's West-end clubs; Mr. Bodley's churches at Cambridge and Hayward's-Heath; Bridgewater-house; and Wren's churches generally'. With this devastating summing-up of his critics, Keeling at once showed the morass into which Victorian architectural criticism had fallen, and indeed in which architectural critics have been wallowing ever since.

Thereafter, so accurate had been his counter-attack, Bassett Keeling was assailed on every possible occasion by the moralists, and, apart from one or two enthusiasts such as Pepperell, all denounced him and his works. His reputation as a church architect was destroyed, and this intelligent and very original designer ceased to figure among the prominent of his day.

However, during the 1860s, Keeling, a member of the Low Church party, had designed and built several churches in London, among which may be mentioned the extraordinary St Mark's, Notting Hill (completed 1863), St George's, Campden Hill (1865), and St Paul's, Upper Norwood (1866). These display several characteristics found in the Music Hall, for Keeling was not a man to divorce the profane from the sacred, especially when counteracting the march of popery.

St Mark's was built by Dove Brothers of Islington, to whom I am indebted for permission to reproduce Keeling's original drawings. The contract was for

£6,011, including fittings, and the church was consecrated by the Bishop of London on 27 November 1863.[12] St Mark's had attracted the attention of the architectural journals, for in November 1862 *The Builder* described it as a 'Gothic structure, in coloured bricks and Bath stone, with a continental touch in it'.[13] The barbaric, emphatic, spiky design was presented for the approval of the members of the Ecclesiological Society, but it was not such as the committee could sanction. The spacious interior, with its lofty arcades of striped brickwork carried on cast-iron columns originally illuminated in strong polychromatic decoration, was skeletal in character. The notched edges of the principal timbers of the nave, and the harsh, uncompromising use of coloured bricks, produced an angular effect, so that the *Leitmotif* was more akin to Zulu war-shields than to anything the Gothic Revival produced elsewhere. The strangely sinister gallery fronts are worthy of notice, and the magpie polychromy of the structure is quite startling. St Mark's was later denounced in *The Building News* as an 'atrocious specimen of coxcombry in architecture'.[14] (Plates 15 and 17.)

St George's, Campden Hill, was noted as being in course of erection in *The Building News* of 29 January 1864,[15] the style being 'continental Gothic, freely treated'. This time the contractors were Myers of Lambeth. Like St Mark's, St George's was a weird Gothic, with nave arcades of coloured brick voussoirs, notched at the arrises, and carried on cast-iron columns decorated in strong polychromy. The interior of the church was faced with yellow stock bricks relieved with blue, red, and black bricks and Bath and Red Mansfield stone. William Pepperell could think of no church where the iron was better treated, for the detail was 'sharp and clear' and the columns did not appear so slender as to look 'unequal to their task of supporting the brick arches and clerestorey'. He particularly admired the nave roof with its 'saw-tooth cut and intersection ribs'.[16] The light, elegant galleries were praised by contemporaries, and the church was described as one of the most successful efforts of the 'modern school of Eclectic Gothic, and though perhaps a little free in treatment, evidences an appreciation of . . . continental Gothic which is not too common'.[17] Like St Mark's, St George's is an expression of an aggressive and barbaric style which Keeling evolved. It was an original design, especially in the use of structure and colour.

St Paul's, Anerley Road, Upper Norwood, was reported in *The Builder* of 11 August 1866[18] as having been consecrated by the Bishop of Winchester. The style was 'French Gothic, freely treated', and the nave arcades were again carried on cast-iron columns coloured blue, green, and black. The nave timbers were treated with lines and stencilled patterns in oil polychromy from the architect's designs. The entire interior, including the solid chancel screen of heroic proportions, was covered in stencilled designs by the architect, and the effect was superbly rich (plate 17). Dove Brothers were again the contractors. The gallery supports are particularly interesting examples of Keeling's functional approach to design. The drawing shows the cast-iron columns and robust timber treatment so characteristic of his work (figs 3a and b).

St Mark's was closed in 1971, but alterations, such as the removal of the galleries and the flying buttresses, and the casing-in of the cast-iron columns, carried out some years before, had left it but a shadow of its former self. St George's suffered even more, the spire being demolished after the war of 1939-45, the interior whitened, the columns cased in, and the apse demolished. St Paul's was in superlative condition up until 1971, when it was closed.

Less extraordinary, yet interesting, designs are St Andrew's, Peckham (still in use), and the Wesleyan Chapel, Dalston (demolished). St Andrew's had marble columns instead of the usual cast iron, but, unbelievably, the whole interior, including the marble, has been painted over.[19] Keeling displayed a remarkable facility for a functional approach to design. His columns were for the most part of cast iron, and therefore capable of production in quantity. He achieved his architectural effects by simple means: contrasted coloured bricks or stones; stencilled patterns, or simple saw cuts in timber. His liking for angles of 45° or 60° and 30° is clearly easy to interpret on site, and very much geared to unsophisticated operatives actually carrying out the job. Thus, using factory methods, repetitive designs, and ultra-simple joinery, Keeling achieved the richest of effects, which may not have been truly 'medieval', but which attained a character of some interest at a fraction of the cost of the buildings of his more acceptable ecclesiologist-minded contemporaries. An examination of the stencilled patterns and the joinery of St Paul's Church, Penge, prove this point (plates 18 and 19).

Keeling became rather elusive in the 1870s. He resigned from the RIBA in 1872, probably because his work was scorned by the purists. He was involved in several cases for recovery of fees, but he does not surface again until 1880. One of the most interesting of Keeling's later buildings was illustrated in *The Builder* of 14 August 1880. This was No 16 Tokenhouse Yard, Lothbury. It was constructed throughout 'in the most substantial manner', and was faced in red sandstone and kiln-burnt red bricks. Important questions of rights of light necessitated the exercise of 'considerable ingenuity in the arrangement and construction', and the staircase was stepped back on each floor, with completely glazed landings to admit as much light as possible. In order to increase the amount of light penetrating the building, Keeling used expanses of white-glazed bricks to face the back elevations which reflected light, a similar treatment to that he gave to Tokenhouse Buildings. In 1880 Keeling is described as being 'of Weavers' Hall'. In the January of 1882 he was elected a Fellow of the Surveyors' Institu-

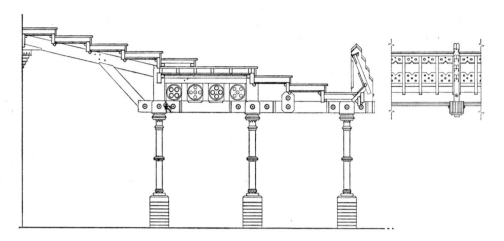

Fig 3a   *Church of St Paul, Anerley Road, London. The gallery structure as designed by E. Bassett Keeling. Drawing by John J. Sambrook*

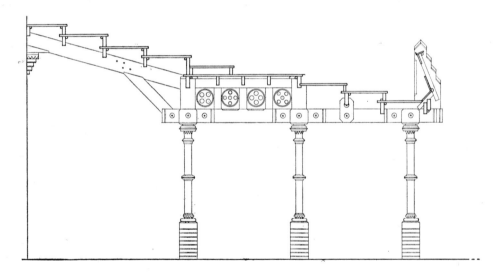

Fig 3b   *Church of St Paul, Anerley Road, London. The gallery structure as executed. Keeling's working drawings are often found to be modified by the builders or by the Clerk of Works. These 'before and after' drawings are based on Keeling's original working drawings in the possession of Dove Brothers of Islington, and kindly made available by them for study. The information was completed by measurements taken of the modified executed design. Drawing by John J. Sambrook*

tion, one of his sponsors being Charles Barry. He seems suddenly to have had a turn in his fortunes, for he built the 'White House', Telegraph St, off Moorgate, which was described in *The British Architect* of 12 October 1883[20] as likely to 'excite surprise and pleasure on a first acquaintance'. It had an entirely white frontage executed in 'Burmantofts' faience. In 1882 Keeling's designs for Token-house Buildings, Lothbury, were realised by Dove Brothers, and Keeling moved his office there, to no 2. This development was extraordinary for its date, being ultra-simple in elevational treatment, and with a light well in the centre faced with white glazed bricks. The starkness of the architecture seems to place it some twenty years before its time, and it is a very progressive building for its date.

In December 1882, however, Keeling's wife died, aged 41, of a haemorrhage after the birth of a son, Bassett Keeling, who followed her to the grave in 1884, aged 1 year 5 months. Keeling redoubled his professional efforts, and a spate of office and residential building resulted. The largest of these schemes was Princes Mansions in Victoria Street, Westminster, containing 'flats for the aristocratic and affluent classes'. The development was 311ft long and 90ft high, consisting of eight floors (plate 29). The elevations were of red brick and 'Lasselles's patent concrete'. Floors were sound-proof and fire-proof. The site has recently been completely redeveloped.[21]

This appears to have been Keeling's last and largest scheme. He died of cirrhosis of the liver, after haematemesis lasting 36 hours, on 30 October 1886, aged 49, at his home, No 5 Paradise Row (now Stoke Newington Church Street). He was buried in grave no 72467, Section L9, in Abney Park Cemetery, with Mary Newby Keeling and young Bassett.[22] He left £209 0s 6d, and letters of administration were granted to his son, Gilbert Thompson Keeling, Architect. It seems that everything connected with Enoch Bassett Keeling was doomed. Few of his works survive, and these are for the most part mutilated. His detractors have triumphed. His home, Dunwood House, 5 Paradise Row, Clissold Park, has been demolished, and even his gravestone has been destroyed. His last resting-place could not be located, even with the help of the cemetery attendants, in March 1971. Poor Bassett Keeling seems destined for complete oblivion, so it is hoped that this brief chapter will serve to recall to students of the Victorian era a very extraordinary and inventive architect.[23, 24]

Notes to this chapter are on page 117

CHAPTER 5

New Technology and Victorian Traffic Relief

That was a happy day, before the days of architects, before the days of builders!

(*Felix illud saeculum ante architectos fuit, ante tectores*)

Seneca, *Epistulae ad Lucilium,* epis 90, sec 9

I have touched on the excellence of good, straightforward design in the structures of the Industrial Revolution already. I stressed the importance of a living tradition found in vernacular architecture, an understanding of the value of craftsmanship, and of a feeling for materials, even new ones. The intelligent empirical experiments with cast iron and other new materials to solve the difficult problems of the day were characteristic of an age of practical men.

The type of structure developed in churches and mills is found in many other buildings. The design for public baths in Leeds by Henry Walker, Architect, shows an essentially ecclesiastical building, with clerestoreyed nave and galleried aisles. Although the structure is mostly timber, the columns are all of cast iron (plate 20). There are many examples of similar construction which may be found in the country, but often the timber is replaced by cast iron. The railway termini offer examples, but so do market halls, public buildings and exhibition buildings. The Covent Garden Fruit Halls set within the Fowler Building are freestanding, built of semi-circular iron ribs on cast-iron columns, and the usual tie-bars are dispensed with. It is true that the first railway sheds were constructed of timber, but this material deteriorated rapidly in the atmosphere of a busy station, and it was soon superseded by iron (plate 21). By 1850 iron was in general use, and at New Street Station, Birmingham, a clear span of 212ft was achieved. Cast iron, so successful in 1851, was also used to great effect in the later exhibitions, notably that of 1862 in Kensington. One of the halls was known as the 'Brompton Boilers', as its appearance from outside was hardly prepossessing, being clad in corrugated iron painted in white and green stripes. The 'Boilers' were demolished and re-erected at Bethnal Green, where they stand to this day, although the halls are clad in brickwork, and they are reduced in area and volume. The elegance of the light, galleried halls may be judged from the picture (plate 22).

Cast iron was also used to produce façades of buildings, notably those of James Bogardus in New York; of John Baird, R. McConnel, William Lochhead, H. Barclay and A. Watt, John Honeyman and James Thomson in Glasgow; and of Peter Ellis in Liverpool. While most of these buildings are spectacular examples, several storeys high, sometimes with complete Orders of architecture, there were plenty of examples throughout Victorian times where cast iron was used for shop-fronts. A charming example is found in Witney, Oxfordshire, in the form of a five-bay front to an ironmonger's shop. The cast-iron columns have idiosyncratic capitals supporting a patterned frieze over which is a painted fascia crowned by a simple Gothic railing (plate 23). James Silk Buckingham was an early enthusiast of cast iron, and he mentions work by 'Mr Laycock of Liverpool' and a pamphlet by Mr Alexander Gordon in his book *National Evils and Practical Remedies with the Plan of a Model Town* (1849), 195-6. Both these references predate *Cast Iron Buildings* by James Bogardus (1856).

While experiments helped to create new systems, and the technology of cast iron came into its own, other traditions of simple, functional design were maintained. Timber had been a familiar material from early times, and fine timber structures are found in many English towns dating from the Middle Ages. However, a functional vernacular tradition of timber building also existed, and Mistley in Essex offers several good specimens. Tall, cavernous streets of timber-boarded warehouses, and maltings of good red bricks capped with slated roofs surrounded by clapboarded vents form unforgettable visual experiences (plate 24).[1] The architecture of the brewing, shipbuilding and cotton industries is full of object lessons in good functional design. The water-fronts of most ports have warehouses and wharves of excellent quality, where the simplest solutions to design problems produce an aesthetic of their own. Consider the problem of getting heavy loads from a warehouse to a street or a quayside. The solution consists of the provision of double doors to each floor opening inwards, with folding platforms outside supported on cast-iron hinges and chains. A jib and pulleys above ensures the easy vertical movement of goods (plate 25).

The elevational treatment of early Victorian and eighteenth-century industrial buildings is of great interest, as simplicity is the keynote. Brickwork is pierced by openings spanned by gauged-brick arches. Corners are formed of blue bull-nosed engineering bricks, both for aesthetic punctuation and for protection. Wall-tie ends of cast iron are permitted to add to the elevational interest (plate 26). Openings, ironwork, fixtures and platforms combine to form a distinctive, functional aesthetic (plate 27).

Something of the same robust approach to design may be discerned in the scheme for 'Metropolitan Traffic Relief', an early Victorian notion for placing all heavy transport in underground roads, leaving the surface free for buses and pedestrians. The system of underground doors to cellars should be noted, as should the gas-lighting, and placing of other services such as telegraph-wires and water-pipes on the walls in as accessible positions as possible. The structure owes much to late eighteenth-century warehouses and factories, for it consists of brick vaulting carried on cast-iron tee-sections supported on cast-iron brackets that also carry the service trunking (plate 30).

Another extraordinary scheme proposed for the 'London Railway' by James Clephan, Architect, and William Curtis, Engineer, shows a public transport system carried on cast-iron arcading above pavement level, shopping being provided under the railway. It will be noted that the proposers do not support steam as the means of power (plate 31). Brunel had promoted a railway powered by a vacuum tube. Unfortunately, he only had leather as a substance at the top of the vacuum tube, and this was most unsatisfactory, being subject to perishing and damage by rodents. Other forms of continuously powered railways were suggested, in which chains or hawsers were attached to the trains and driven on a centrally placed steam-engine. Electric power would, of course, have been ideal for such schemes, but some fifty years were to elapse before development of that energy was provided on the necessary scale.

When the use of the electric telegraph became general, it was found necessary to establish in all large towns branch stations, from which messages were conveyed to the central station, or to which they were sent, either by messenger or by telegraph. The latter had the disadvantage of increasing the possibility of error, while the former was necessarily slow. This problem led to the invention of a system for propelling, by air pressure, the messages themselves through tubes that connected the stations. This was first developed by the Electric and International Telegraph Company, which connected its central station in London with the City branch stations. The apparatus was designed and built by Clark and Varley in 1854. The first tube laid down was from Lothbury, scene of Bassett Keeling's later triumphs, and the Stock Exchange. The tube had an inside diameter of $1\frac{1}{2}$in, but a larger tube was later laid between Telegraph Street and Mincing Lane. The principle of locomotion was to propel the carriers by atmospheric pressure, a vacuum having first been created in the direction of travel by pumping out the air. The later development of compressing the air behind the carrier produced a gain of speed, and got over the problems caused by the creation of a vacuum, including the sucking of water into the tube through the joints in the pipes. This water sometimes accumulated to such a degree that it overcame the power of the vacuum to draw the air through. Later technical improvements in jointing and the development of syphonic systems to remove water helped the vacuum method. The construction of the carriers was also a tricky problem to be solved pragmatically. Gutta-percha, papier-maché covered with felt, and iron pipes lined with lead were tried.

Siemens laid tubes for the General Post Office in 1869 in order to connect the GPO and the Central Telegraph Station, and by that time proposals were being put forward for pneumatic power to propel the trains in the proposed Channel Tunnel, but further experiment indicated that the system would require enormous power at a central plant as well as creating technical difficulties that the age was not capable of solving. There is no doubt that the Victorians could have constructed the Channel Tunnel, and that within a few years they could have produced electric trains to run within it. The economic disasters of the 1870s together with the collapse of France in 1871 shelved the project.

When the traffic in the streets of London became excessive, it was decided to lay a new railway under the surface of the normal thoroughfares. The London Underground Railway was constructed over a period of three years, and was opened for traffic in 1863. The line began at Paddington, and originally terminated at Moorgate. The majority of the stations were open to the sky, but Baker Street and Gower Street were completely under ground, with roofs formed of arched brickwork immediately below the streets. The use of glazed bricks and white tiles helped to reflect light, thus reducing the amount of gas-light necessary, as well as helping maintenance and cleaning. The construction of the retaining walls is interesting. There are piers 10ft apart between which are vertical arches to resist the thrust of the earth. The tops of the piers are connected by arches, and thus it was possible not only to resist the pressure of the earth on either side of the excavated area, but to carry the structures overhead. Although this railway was constructed on the 'cut and fill' basis, it fitted within the fabric of London with remarkable neatness compared with the enormous wastes created by modern roadworks. Later on, the 'tube' system got over the problems of fitting a new transport route within a built-up city to an even greater extent.[2]

The scheme by Clephan and Curtis is of enormous interest in that it shows the care with which attempts were made to make the vast engineering works aesthetically and practically acceptable. The railway is integrated within the street, and does not tear the fabric of the town apart.

Other proposals show how the skills of Regency architects and the concern for the quality of architectural treatment of cities were carried forward into the reigns of William IV and Victoria. The plans for a viaduct for the Westminster and Deptford Railway by the architect I. D. Paine show a sumptuously treated underside of a railway viaduct decorated with Roman and Greek motifs. Shopfronts are set between the supporting piers, with delightful façades recalling the work of J. B. Papworth to mind, and the picture is one of elegance, with something of the stylishness of Burlington Arcade (plate 32). It contrasts with the miles of stock-brick viaducts that carry the railway to Deptford and Greenwich from London Bridge and Waterloo. Yet even these high-level railways left large areas free for the insertion of stores, warehouses, and sometimes even dwellings underneath the viaducts, which could be let to private individuals. Generally, however, the effect of Victorian brick viaducts has something of the grandeur of Roman engineering works (plate 28). One of the best examples is the great bricked ramped viaduct carrying the road from the harbour at Ramsgate (plate 35). This noble edifice is designed with the powerful rhythm of arches, roundels, and massive keystones playing their parts in a truly heroic work. Large warehouse units are provided under this viaduct, and the façade to the harbour quays is crowned by a massive brick cornice capped by a balustrade.

Often, classical motifs are simplified, interpreted and applied with boldness to a design problem. The bridge carrying the railway from Southwark to Cannon Street Station in London is a case in point, for here, massive, vaguely Doric columns carry the great bridge, the effect having a grandeur and strength that is not common today but was often a hallmark of Victorian work (plate 33).

In other cases the desire to apply Gothic frippery to a structure became too strong, and the curious 'Design for the Ornamentation of Lambeth Bridge' by the architect E. C. Robins demonstrates something of the difficulties into which the Victorians sometimes got themselves (plate 34). The welter of Puginesque detail, however, was proposed for a reason: the desire to match the style of the Palace of Westminster and also to respect the ancient Lambeth Palace. Despite Mr Robins's odd adaptation of the piers of a suspension bridge to resemble a cross between Nonsuch and the Houses of Parliament, it cannot be denied that the bridge is still expressed as of the suspension variety, while the very light Gothic detail of the piers and of the balustrades is charming in its way.

However, the integrity of the unselfconscious examples illustrated and described in this chapter contrast favourably with Mr Robins's design.

The limitations of early Victorian engineering were already apparent by 1847 when Robert Stephenson's Dee Bridge collapsed under a train. The trussed cast-iron girders were too brittle to withstand the considerable stresses caused by vibration. The development of steel was a result of the work of Bessemer and the Siemens Brothers, but Britain lagged behind Europe in its use. The engineer Barlow noted that steel had been used for structural purposes in the United States, but its similar use was 'obstructed by some deficiency in our own arrangements, and by the absence of suitable regulations from the Board of Trade . . .'. As with many reforms in Britain, it needed a disaster to blast bureaucracy from its slumberbed of idleness and complacency. Like cholera in the 1840s, which had been responsible for reforms in sewerage and the provision of drinking water, as well as for solving the problems of burying the dead, wind-pressure was to bring about a number of deaths. Only after death and disaster, apparently, can an essentially unimaginative and pig-headed Establishment be persuaded to act. We would not have had a Clean Air Act had not the deaths from smog reached epidemic proportions, and we certainly shall not begin to control the advance of the motor car until something more dramatic than statistical death-rates can be shown.

The disaster which gave the impetus to the encouragement of the use of steel in building had its origins in the competition for passenger traffic to Scotland. Two great railways had been built. The difficulties of the route to Cumberland and Westmorland were considerable, but north of the border it was comparatively easy country once Shap had been negotiated. The east-coast companies had a clear run to Yorkshire, but the Tyne, the Forth, and the Tay offered only miserably slow ferry connections, so in order to improve matters, bridges were proposed. The Tyne was bridged in 1849, but it was not until the 1870s that

Thomas Bouch was commissioned to bridge the Tay and the Forth. Bouch chose a structure of wrought-iron lattice girders supported on cast-iron structures standing on brick and stone bases for the bridge over the Tay, and the enormous feat was completed in 1878, to the praises of William McGonagall, poet and tragedian, who declared it to be the 'greatest wonder of the day'. However, on 'the last Sabbath day of 1879, which will be remembered for a very long time', ninety lives were lost when the Edinburgh express travelling north plunged down into the river during a storm. McGonagall tells the story thus:

> *So the train mov'd slowly along the Bridge of Tay,*
> *Until it was about midway,*
> *Then the central girders with a crash gave way,*
> *And down went the train and passengers into the Tay!*
> . . . . .
> *And the cry rang out o'er the town,*
> *Good Heavens! the Tay Bridge is blown down . . .*

The poet makes some pertinent observations on the construction of the bridge, although in his previous epic on the opening of the bridge, he wished 'prosperity to Messrs. Bouch and Grothe, the famous engineers':

> *I must conclude my lay*
> *By telling the world fearlessly without the least dismay,*
> *That your central girders would not have given away,*
> *At least many sensible men do say,*
> *Had they been supported on each side with buttresses,*
> *At least many sensible men confesses,*
> *For the stronger we our houses do build,*
> *The less chance we have of being killed.*

Buttresses, however (*pace* McGonagall), were not the remedy. At an inquiry it was found that the bridge had been 'badly designed, badly constructed and badly maintained and that its downfall was due to inherent defects in the structure which must sooner or later have brought it down. For these defects . . . Sir Thomas Bouch is . . . mainly to blame.' The defects appear to have been mainly due to a gross underestimation of the maximum wind pressures likely to bear on the bridge. This underestimation appears to have been due to the advice of the Astronomer Royal who dogmatised on most matters, but in this case pronounced that the greatest wind pressure was not likely to exceed 10 lbs per square foot. Bouch was, however, ruined, and work on his plans for the Forth Bridge was at

Illustrations

1 *The Mill at Shipley Glen, Saltaire, near Bradford, Yorkshire, in 1860. This vast factory, built of light brown stone in the Italianate manner, was completed in 1853 for (Sir) Titus Salt. The architects were Lockwood and Mawson. The building is 550ft long and six storeys high. The floors were designed to be carried on brick arches springing from ornamented cast-iron beams. The chimney, like a great campanile, is 250ft high, and was carefully constructed to contain 'Green and Twibell's patent fuel economizers' to remove 'annoying effluvium'. William Fairbairn, in his On the Application of Cast and Wrought Iron to Building Purposes, published in 1857, observed that 'Mr. Salt, with that forethought and liberality which are absolutely essential to the successful and profitable working of all such concerns, determined that it should embody the results of the newest inventions and the most perfect construction'. The factory was opened in 1853, a banquet being provided for two and a half thousand workers and over a thousand other guests. The Earl of Harewood, who attended the feast, opined that he had developed a high notion of the manufacturing classes as a result of his visit. It is interesting to imagine what the Crystal Palace would have looked like had Salt purchased it to house his 'Works', as he once intended, in the setting of Shipley Glen*

THIS AQUEDUCT
was erected by
THE STRATFORD CANAL COMP.Y
in October. 1813.
BERNARD DEWES Esq.R CHAIRMAN.
W. JAMES Esq.R DEP.Y CHAIRMAN
W. WHITMORE ENGINEER

2 *Detail of the Aqueduct at Wootton Wawen, Warwickshire. 'The aqueducts on the Stratford canal are beautiful examples of cast-iron construction, with their standard railings, trough sections bolted together, and simple brick supports.' The aqueduct was constructed in 1813. The aesthetic sense of the designers was faultless*

The exterior of
Barton Arcade, Manchester

4 (above) *The domed roof of the Barton Arcade, Deansgate, Manchester, designed by Corby, Raby and Sawyer, using a 'Kit-of-Parts' cast at Macfarlane's Saracen Foundry in Glasgow*

5 (right) *Roof of the Barton Arcade, Deansgate, Manchester, showing the delicate filigree effects obtained by mass-produced ironwork. The elegance of this example should be compared with some contemporary crudities*

6 (below) 'The warehouses by the Thames are simple, functional answers' to the problem of storage and of the transfer of materials from a ship to dry land. Materials are used in an utterly unaffected way, and the cranes are mounted with engaging directness to the sides of the buildings. Although the classical traditions are observed, Gothic influences are just apparent in this example

7 (above) St Pancras Station. 'The details of the junctions between the shed and the brickwork are simply achieved . . .' This magnificent iron-work, made by the Butterly Company of Derbyshire in 1867, obeys classical principles

8 (left) *St Pancras Station. 'Its girders join the Gothic brickwork in a satisfying rhythm, and the whole is a great piece of functional design, the elements of which are completely clear.' Those who consider the train shed and the brickwork to be unrelated should study this and the preceding plate. It will be quickly seen that the conventional wisdom based on the received idea that the 'architecture' and the 'engineering' do not merge in St Pancras is sheer nonsense*

9 (below) *Detail of part of Holborn Viaduct, spanning Farringdon Street. 'The architectural details of the Viaduct are handled superbly well, the granite columns and cast-iron arches with delicate decorations adding to the richness of London's fabric'*

10 (below) 'Proposed High Level Road and Viaduct from St Sepulchre's Church to Hatton Garden.' A scheme by the architect F. Marrable published by Cundall, Downes and Co as a forerunner of Holborn Viaduct. Note how the space under the viaduct was to be used for elegant shops, and how the high-level road was to be developed in conjunction with grand, unified façades of shops and apartments. A comparison with contemporary lack of thought given to the undersides of elevated motorways should be soberly considered

11 (bottom) 'Birds Eye View of the London Grand Junction Railway from Skinner Street to Camden Town' drawn by George Remington, Junior, and lithographed by Bouvier. The publisher was G. S. Tregear. This scheme shows the bold way in which Victorian railway viaducts were visualised as fitting into the fabric of cities. The ultra-simple grand staircase flanked by two gaslights and the ornamental gate are hardly what we could imagine as a railway terminus, but there is something noble in the directness of the intention

12
(left) 'The open stairs and access galleries ... were purely functional in design.' Easily washed down, and permanently ventilated, these staircases were a considerable advance on enclosed timber stairs in tenements. Excrement, vomit, urine and vermin were more easily removed, while suffocating stenches were avoided

13 (right) 'Alfred Waterhouse's magnificent Gothic Revival Town Hall' was not only conveniently planned and harmoniously composed, but symbolised the new pride of young, striving, vigorous Manchester. It is among the greatest monuments of Victorian Gothic architecture

14

(above) *Sectional view of the interior of The Strand Music Hall, London, by Enoch Bassett Keeling '...a veritable Aladdin's cave of entertainment architecture', the hall was lighted through the ceiling which was composed of coloured glass set in a metal frame. Over a thousand glass prisms reflected the gaslight, and refracted the colours of the spectrum to add to the riot of detail*

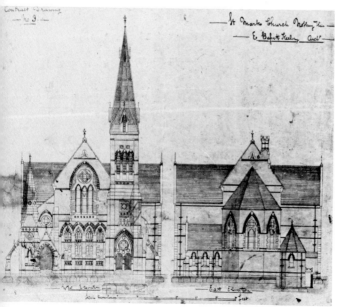

15

(left) *E. Bassett Keeling's original elevational drawings for the church of St Mark, Notting Hill, London. The incredibly thin and skeletal flying buttresses with the mawkish piling together of eclectic forms are typical of Keeling at his most rasping*

16 *The exterior of The Strand Music Hall, London. The design 'exhibits all the angular spikiness so characteristic of E. Bassett Keeling's early work'. Note the polychrome brick voussoirs and the iron decoration contributing to the aggressive qualities of the architecture*

17 (right) *E. Bassett Keeling's original detail drawing for the church of St Mark, Notting Hill, London. Note the curious gallery fronts, notched timbers and brickwork, especially the spindly flying buttress. The treatment of the cast-iron capitals, with 'trays' from which the arcade springs should be compared with similar details in the church of St Paul, Anerley Road (below). Keeling sought to suggest rich 'Gothic' effects by the simplest and cheapest means, including 45° saw-cuts, notched brickwork, filigree cast-iron work, and wildly polychrome brickwork*

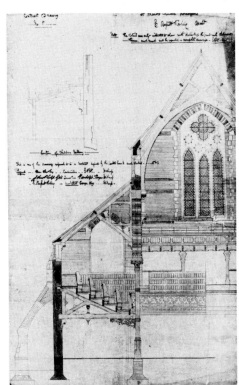

18 (below) *St Paul's Church, Anerley Road, London. 'The entire interior . . . was covered in stencilled designs by the architect, and the effect was superbly rich.' Note the cast-iron columns with their oddly 'Moresque' character rather like lacework at the point where the columns carry 'trays' to support the arcade*

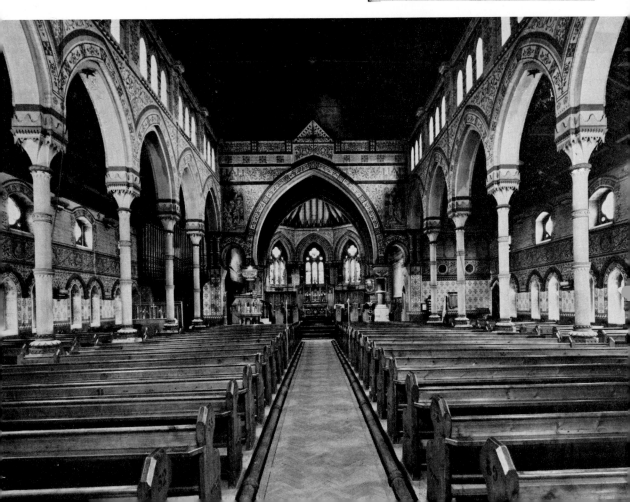

19 *St Paul's Church, Anerley Road, London. 'The gallery supports are particularly interesting examples of Keeling's functional approach to design.' Timber and cast iron are used simply, the richness achieved by stencilled patterns and by elementary carpentry*

Public Baths in Leeds by Henry Walker, Architect. This is a good example of a timber structure based on traditional prototypes carried on cast-iron columns to cover a large space

21

(right) *London Bridge Station, showing the sophisticated iron structure of a Victorian railway terminus where large spaces had to be roofed using a minimum number of columns. The elegant designs in the spandrels of the arches should be noted. War damage has revealed the structure clearly*

22

(below) *The interior of the Bethnal Green Museum, formerly part of the exhibition complex at Brompton, and originally known as the 'Brompton Boilers' owing to the utilitarian appearance of the sheds*

23 *Cast-iron shop-front in Witney, Oxfordshire. Similar fronts exist in Witney, and comprise a kit-of-parts of columns, brackets, fascia and balcony rail*

24 'Tall, cavernous streets of timber-boarded warehouses and maltings of good red bricks
   capped with slated roofs surmounted by clapboarded vents form unforgettable visual
   experiences' and are part of a great tradition of functional buildings found in Essex.
   The examples are in Mistley

25

(opposite) *Warehouse in Southwark, showing the double doors, folding platforms, and jib. Nothing could be simpler or more effective for the job than this arrangement*

26

(left) *'Brickwork is pierced by openings spanned by gauged-brick arches. Corners are formed of blue bull-nosed engineering bricks, both for aesthetic punctuation and for protection. Wall-tie ends of cast iron are permitted to add to the elevational interest.'*

(right) *'Openings, ironwork, fixtures and platforms combine to form a distinctive, functional aesthetic.'*

28 *Victorian brick viaducts have something of the grandeur of Roman engineering works about them. This example is at Windsor, Berkshire*

29 (top) *Princes Mansions, Victoria Street, Westminster, by E. Bassett Keeling, containing 'flats for the aristocratic and affluent classes'. This shows Keeling's 1880's style—somewhat Frenchified, hardly beautiful, and markedly aggressive.*

30 (bottom) *A scheme for 'Metropolitan Traffic Relief'. Note how the Victorians thought of separating heavy goods traffic from lighter passenger needs. Their sense of scale and proportion was rather better than ours*

31 *A scheme for the 'London Railway' by Clephan and Curtis. This is a remarkable piece of integrated architecture, planning, and transport. The railways were to be run on a vacuum-suction principle, or by compressed air, using pneumatic tubes. Electric power was equally feasible. Problems of vibration and noise, however, would have been difficult to overcome, but would be technically possible to defeat today. The contemporary dilemma would be in the creation of an aesthetically comparable scheme*

32 (above) *A perspective of the underside of a viaduct carrying the Westminster and Deptford Railway, by I. D. Paine. We have never thought out the problems of what to do with the spaces under motorways. The Victorians designed all sorts of schemes for using the spaces under their railways, and this is a splendid example*

33 (overleaf) *'Often, classical motifs are simplified, interpreted, and applied with boldness to a design problem.' The bridge over the Thames from Southwark to Cannon Street Station is a case in point*

Design for the Ornamentation of

Lambeth Bridge

G. G. Robins Esq Architect F.R.I.B.A.

35 (above) *One of the best examples of Victorian brick viaducts is the great ramp carrying the road up from the harbour at Ramsgate, Kent. The splendid quality of the brickwork, and the fact that the viaduct is an asset in civic design terms, are obvious. The spaces under the viaduct are used, and the whole thing has been well thought out*

34 (left) *A 'Design for the Ornamentation of Lambeth Bridge' by the architect E. C. Robins. This is a curious Gothic invention, presumably to harmonise stylistically with Lambeth Palace and the Palace of Westminster*

36 (above) *The Gin Shop. An etching by George Cruikshank, dated 1 November 1829. Although highly moralistic in tone, the beginnings of Gin Palace décor can be discerned in the 'marbled' pilasters, display of casks (caricatured as caskets), and marble-topped bar*

37

(below left) *An etching by George Cruikshank in the series* The Drunkard's Children *showing an early Gin Palace interior. The ornate gas lamps and the flares, the plate-glass windows, the mirrors, and the display of casks add up to a suitably grand interior in great contrast to the drabness outside*

38

(right) *The Crown Liquor Saloon, Belfast. 'The startling richness of lettered advertisements, mirrors, a tiled long bar with a marble counter-top, painted and etched glass, and fine woods, give us some idea of what the true Gin Palace was like'*

39

(below) *The Crown Liquor Saloon, Belfast. 'The entrance doors possess splendidly robust door furniture with pull-handles, push-bars, and engraved plates.' This door furniture was supremely functional, designed to stand up to hard knocks and a great deal of use. Note the 'grained' wood, varnished to give a hard-wearing surface*

40

(left) *'The Citadel', a Gin Palace with Gothic pretentions in its detail, in Belfast. The privacy screen has an ecclesiastical flavour somewhat reminiscent of the confessional. The mirror-advertisement boasts that 'The Citadel' sells only one quality 'of liquors —THE BEST'. Note the casks, the Lincrusta ceiling, and the general richness of the interior*

41

(right) *The Leadenhall Market, City of London, by the City Architect, Sir Horace Jones. Here, iron and glass roofs are carried on giant Ionic columns. The rich maroon and gold livery gives the Market a marvellous dignity. Not only is the Market a civilised place in which to shop under cover, but it provides refreshments in the capacious pubs, one of which (The Lamb) retains its etched plate-glass windows and tiled basement*

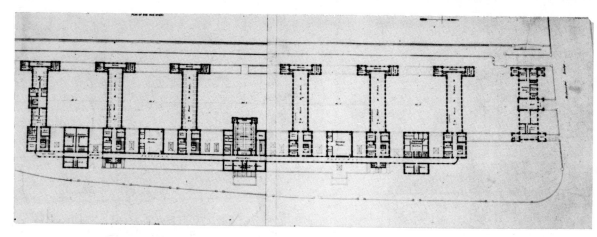

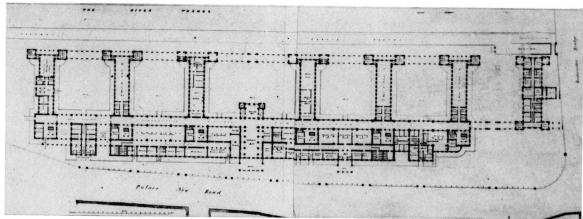

42 (above) *Plan of St Thomas's Hospital, London. The 'pavilion' principle is well demon-strated in this plan, and wards are separated from each other, though linked by corridors*

43 (below) *Perspective view of St Thomas's Hospital, Lambeth, London. This fine Italianate group of buildings was designed by Henry Currey and was completed in 1870-1. The plan was considered perfect when it was first built, and the hospital as a whole was thought to be an addition to the metropolis that would not be surpassed in appearance. A comparison with the new buildings (1972) now replacing Currey's work is sufficient to make the truth of the latter statement devastatingly apparent*

4 (above) *South-east view of Wormwood Scrubs Prison showing the boundary wall and a typical cell building. Staircases, vents, and sanitary stacks were expressed in the building, and the completed prison combines the direct integrity familiar from early warehouse and industrial buildings with a mildly Romanesque concession to fenestration and detail. Reproduced from a photograph of* circa 1883

5 (below) *The St Charles Hospital, North Kensington. This photolitho from* The Builder *of 25 June 1881 shows the whole complex of buildings designed on the 'pavilion' principle by H. Saxon Snell & Son. In the background may be seen a very inaccurate representation of the Anglican chapel at Kensal Green Cemetery designed in 1836 by J. W. Griffith. The Great Western Railway may also be seen*

46 *Houses in Lloyd Square, Clerkenwell, London. These were designed in 1819 by John Booth, and erected in the following few years with the co-operation of his son, William Joseph Booth, who became Surveyor to the Drapers' Company. Even when stucco was used sparingly, as in these delightful examples, the problems of maintenance were acute. The civilised scale of nineteenth-century English housing compared with conditions in Europe has long been admired by European commentators*

47
(above) *The almshouses at Saltaire, near Bradford, designed by Lockwood and Mawson. The architects favoured an Italianate style, reminiscent of very small-scale Venetian Gothic*

48
(left) *A late-Victorian lavatory in the City of London, showing the functional materials which were easily washed down and able to stand up to hard wear. The hefty door-furniture, massive porcelain stalls, and glazed-brick walls are ideally suited to the purpose of the building*

49 *Abbey Mills Pumping-Station, design by (Sir) Joseph Bazalgette. 'The various galleries and levels are carried on robust cast-iron columns with foliate capitals.' The simple, almost nautical details of the handrails are in contrast with the ornate ironwork*

50 *Even the floors of the cat-walks at Abbey Mills are composed of beautifully cast geometrical patterns. The functional aspects of this flooring should not be overlooked. The lace-like effect is partly in order to save weight, and the pattern helps to give a sure grip to the soles of shoes. Apart from these considerations, the iron floor is attractive*

51 (above left) *The balustrades of the high-level cat-walks at Abbey Mills are exquisite examples of High Victorian ironwork design. The simple nut-and-bolt fixings ensured that erection on site was quick, but the final effect was rich and interesting*

52 (above right) *The beautiful door-hinges, based on formalised plant-shapes, at Abbey Mills are not only agreeable objects in themselves, but strengthen the wooden door-panels, and thus have a functional purpose. The decorative effects of the notched and chamfered edge of the panel give additional richness as well as avoiding breakages of sharp arrises*

53 (below) *'... the beautiful Kew Palm House', erected 1844-8, by Richard Turner to designs by himself and Decimus Burton*

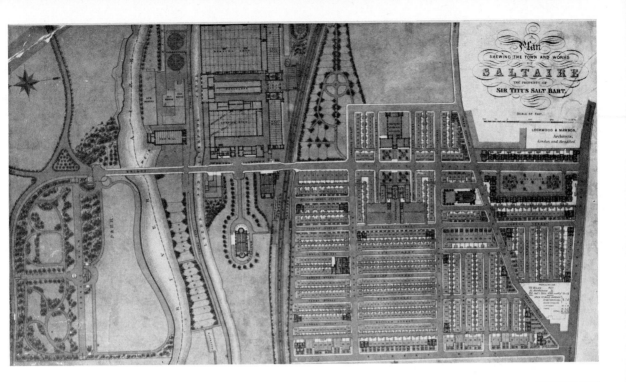

54
(above) 'Plan shewing the town and works of Saltaire, the property of Sir Titus Salt Bart.' This shows the completed township designed by the architects Lockwood and Mawson of Bradford. The advantageous site can at once be appreciated. The River Aire is on the left, and the factory and church lie between the Leeds and Liverpool Canal and the railway tracks. The town itself is laid out on geometrical lines

55
(right) Four Per Cent Industrial Dwellings in the East End, 1889-90. These are typical of the large tenements erected in Whitechapel just after the Jack the Ripper murders

56
(overleaf) Typical dwellings erected by the Peabody Trust in London; this example is near Clerkenwell Green. The walls are massively constructed of grey-brown brick, and the roofs are covered with grey slate

57 *Houses near St Peter's Church in Belfast. 'Artisans' houses had a post-Georgian simplicity', and, despite the poverty and meanness, were always brightly painted. The pieces of pipe fixed to the walls are for holding flags on days of celebration*

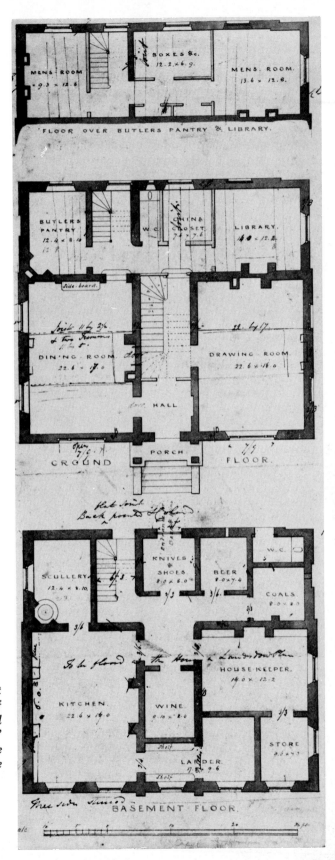

58 *A typical double-fronted house plan of the first half of the nineteenth century. The amount of space given to the storage of beer and wine should be noted, and the organisation of 'back stairs' and main stairs demonstrates the importance given to segregating the 'working' part of the house from the main rooms*

59 (left) *An entrance to a Victorian tenement in Clerkenwell, London. The integrated design of doorway, arch, tympanum, lettering, ironwork, and footscrapers is worthy of note. The stair well is open to light and air*

60 (below) *Percy Circus (partially demolished) on the New River Company's Estate in Clerkenwell, London. 'The spear-headed cast-iron railings . . . will be familiar to many people.' Mass-produced artifacts were made using the classical language of architecture, and helped to hold the townscape together in a homogeneous whole*

61 'The miniature of some North Oxford fantasy is found in Mistley.' This Essex township has some delightful buildings, not least of which is this charming villa in the Gothic manner. The disposition of the rooms is clearly expressed by the exterior, and the building is the antithesis of the symmetrical classical or Italianate houses commonly erected in Victorian times

once stopped.

W. H. Barlow rebuilt the Tay Bridge on new piers of massive solidity compared with Bouch's filigree piers, but transferred Bouch's girders to the new structure, having strengthened them with wrought iron and steel decking. The new bridge was completed in 1887, and McGonagall once more burst into flowery verse:

> *Beautiful new railway bridge of the silvery Tay,*
> *With your strong brick piers and buttresses [sic] in so*
> > *grand array,*
> *And your thirteen central girders, which seem to my eye*
> *Strong enough all windy storms to defy.*

The poet noted further improvements over the old bridge, including the

> *. . . beautiful side-screens along your railway,*
> *Which will be a great protection on a windy day,*
> *So as the railway carriages won't be blown away,*
> *And ought to cheer the hearts of the passengers night and day . . .*

Further, McGonagall noted the new structure with approval, observing that it

> *. . . seems strong and grand,*
> *And the workmanship most skilfully planned;*
> *And I hope the designers, Messrs Barlow and Arrol, will*
> > *prosper for many a day*
> *For erecting thee across the beautiful Tay.*

Although steel was used in the reconstruction of the Tay Bridge, it was not used on the scale of American practice, despite the claim put somewhat chauvinistically by McGonagall that

> *The New Yorkers boast about their Brooklyn Bridge,*
> *But in comparison to thee it seems like a midge . . .*

With this excruciating couplet from the *Poetic Gems* of William McGonagall, we will return to the building of the Forth Bridge, which marked the first great breakthrough in modern steel construction.

Sir John Fowler and Benjamin Baker submitted a design for this railway bridge to replace Bouch's discredited work. The enormous spans and heights at

E

Queensferry posed problems to the engineers which they solved with novel and breathtaking designs. Baker resolved to build the Forth Bridge of steel, and the superior technology of the 1880s enabled enormous plates of steel to be produced from the rolling-mills. The contractors, Messrs Tancred Arrol, had special rolling, planing, and drilling machines installed at Queensferry, and slowly the huge tubes that formed the main members of the structure grew from the piers. The principles of the cantilever were explored in this incomparable work of Victorian engineering, and Fowler remarked that he did not believe in 'astronomy being a safe guide for practical engineering'. The Forth Bridge was opened in 1890.

The newly-knighted Baker was assailed by hostile criticism of the design. It was condemned as the 'supremest specimen of all ugliness', and the unusual shape of the structure caused the aesthetes of Britain to have paroxysms of loathing.

Baker replied in terms which suggested that if the design of the Forth Bridge were judged from the same standpoint as a silver chimney ornament, the exercise would be ludicrous. 'It is impossible,' he said, 'to pronounce authoritatively on the beauty of an object without knowing its functions.' The views of William Morris are particularly interesting, for Morris could only see that every technical improvement was bringing about more and yet more ugliness. He could never accept that there would be an architecture of iron, and thought that every improvement in machinery was uglier and uglier. Morris could only despair at the growing arrogance of man when faced with Nature. The Forth Bridge was for him a symbol of man's mastery over matter and over Nature, and of his growing alienation from his roots.

The steel construction of the Forth Bridge made possible enormous strides in the construction of ships and boilers, and the age of the monster floating transatlantic liner was heralded. The *Kaiser Wilhelm der Grosse*, the *Titanic*, the *Lusitania*, and the *Mauretania* were perhaps the highest achievements of the ocean-going liner builders.

The use of steel was only one aspect of Victorian functional technology. When we think of a Victorian street, we conjure up a vision of great richness, and invoke a world of gas-lamps, cabs, top-hats, and a smoky, foggy quality that is slightly murky and vaguely sinister. The Victorian Age is unthinkable without the hiss of gas-lamps. F. A. Winsor founded the London Gas Light and Coke Company in Regency times, and by the time George IV had ascended the throne, London had over 100 miles of gas-mains. When Victoria became Queen gas-light was established throughout the main towns of the kingdom. The great gas-holders sliding up and down in a framework of superimposed Doric cast-iron columns became an essential feature of the Victorian city.

The advent of electricity was relatively slow, so great were the technical problems. Even so, carbon-arc lamps were installed in lighthouses in the late 1850s, the dynamos being driven by steam power. In the 1870s the inventions of Gramme were adopted by Colonel Crompton, and St Enoch's Station in Glasgow was illuminated by electricity. Crompton's own house was lit by electric light using a generating-set and a steam traction engine. Carbon arcs were not suitable for general domestic use, however, and it was not until Edison and Swan teamed up to found the Edison and Swan United Electric Light Company in 1883 that the possibility of providing electric light on a massive scale became possible, through the development of the filament lamp. However, the dynamos were provided on a local basis, and it was not until Sebastian Ziani de Ferranti developed the concept of the large generating-station at Deptford that the true possibilities of electric power became understood. He planned the distribution of power at pressures and on a scale never before contemplated, and thus may be seen as the father of the modern power-station. Low-pressure direct current was, however, generally preferred, and Ferranti's high-pressure alternating system was obscured, only to re-emerge as the national system later in the twentieth century. The station at Deptford is a massive shed carried on huge purpose-made cast-iron columns, quite functional in design, and very much engineer's architecture, quite different from those pretty cast-iron columns favoured earlier in the century for railway stations, Bassett Keeling churches, and other buildings. Oddly, the walls of Deptford Power Station, of brick, have pointed arches of Gothic ancestry, one of the last hangovers from the Ruskinian influence.

The possibilities that electricity offered for traction were not fully appreciated at first, and the energy was only used for lighting initially. The pneumatic systems were only possible on a small scale, and steam power was therefore the dominant nineteenth-century locomotive source. At the Berlin Exhibition of 1879 Siemens demonstrated a miniature electric engine, and four years later the firm built the electric tramway on the north coast of County Antrim, in Northern Ireland, which pre-dated the pioneer tramway on the front at Brighton. It is a tragedy that this Ulster tramway, with so much of the original rolling-stock, was scrapped after World War II.

Very soon after the Giant's Causeway Tramway, electric power came into use for tramways at Blackpool and Leeds, and electricity was used for the modernisation of the Metropolitan and District Lines, and many railways round London. Deep 'tube' railways became possible with the development of electricity as a source of power, and the difficulties of steam traction underground were overcome.

Notes to this chapter are on page 118

CHAPTER 6

Gin Palaces

Don't tell my mother I'm living in sin
Don't let the old folks know :
Don't tell my twin that I breakfast on gin,
He'd never survive the blow.

A. P. Herbert

Towards the end of the seventeenth century the drinking of beers, ales, and wines as a popular custom became challenged by a new and menacing intoxicant. When William of Orange and Queen Mary arrived from the Netherlands, their Court brought *Jenever* or *Geneva* to London as a fashionable drink.[1] The name became shortened in English usage to *gin,* and 'blue ruin', as the beverage became known, had become a great problem by the time Hogarth produced his famous and savage engravings showing the evil effects of gin-drinking contrasted with the wholesome Englishness of 'Beer-street'.

Gin consumption in the eighteenth and nineteenth centuries had become a real social problem, and the Government, wishing to eliminate the disastrous effects caused by the enormous quantities being drunk by the public, passed a law in 1830 to encourage the drinking of beer. This was to be accomplished by permitting anyone to open an ale-house that could not be licensed for the sale of spirits, and where beer could actually be brewed on the premises. Freed from control by the Justices, over 40,000 beer-shops opened within eight years. The large brewery companies and the owners of public taverns saw the new beer-shops as a great threat to business and began buying up licensed houses, where gin and other strong liquors could be sold. These licensed pubs were converted by the companies and speculators into the grand Victorian Gin Palaces which have been denounced as the source of manifold evils, but which were the result and not the cause of the problem.

Stephen Geary (died 1854) is credited by some authorities with the design of the first Gin Palace, and indeed his eclectic genius was ideally suited to the challenge presented by this new architectural form. Among other works by him were King's Cross (1830) at Battle Bridge (which consisted of a statue of George IV set on a high podium containing first a police station but later a public-house), and Highgate Cemetery.[2] He was the author of a book of designs for tombs and monuments of very remarkable coarseness,[3] and no doubt his zestful pencil was equally at home loosely interpreting classical detail for the embellishment of Gin Palaces. J. B. Papworth is also said to have been the designer of the Original Gin Palace, probably Thompson & Fearons, of 1829-31. Grapes, vine-leaves and pot-bellied *Putti* replaced acanthus-leaves and swags in the new Gin Palace architecture. Whether or not Geary was responsible for the Original Gin Palace, the fashion for bright new pubs began to catch on. Dickens noted in 1835 that

the epidemic began to display itself among the linendrapers and haberdashers. The primary symptoms were an inordinate love of plate-glass, and a passion for gas-lights and gilding . . .—when it burst forth with a ten-fold violence among the publicans, and keepers of 'wine-vaults'. From that moment it has spread among them with unprecedented rapidity, exhibiting a concatenation of all the previous symptoms; onward it has rushed to every part of town, knocking down all the old public-houses, and depositing splendid mansions, stone balustrades, rosewood fittings, immense lamps, and illuminated clocks, at the corner of every street.

In his *Sketches by Boz* he compared the drabness of the poorer quarters of London with the new Gin Palaces:

> You turn the corner. What a change! All is light and brilliancy. The hum of many voices issues from that splendid gin-shop which forms the commencement of the two streets opposite; and the gay building with the fantastically ornamented parapet, the illuminated clock, the plate-glass windows surrounded by stucco rosettes, and the profusion of gas-lights in richly-lit burners, is perfectly dazzling when contrasted with the drabness and dirt we have just left. The interior is even gayer than the exterior. A bar of French-polished mahogany, elegantly carved, extends the whole width of the place; and there are two aisles of great casks, painted green and gold, enclosed within a light brass rail, and bearing such inscriptions as 'Old Tom, 549'; 'Young Tom, 360'; 'Samson, 1421'—, the figures agreeing, we presume, with 'gallons', understand.

Now although we have these descriptions and other contemporary notes, we have to rely on drawings and engravings to establish a true idea of what Gin Palaces were really like. One of the most prolific recorders was George Cruikshank, and we are fortunate in having a caricature from his pen of the Gin Shop in its early stages before it became completely palatial. The moral tone of Cruikshank's drawings is clear, and the devastating effects of gin-drinking were depicted: the paths to the Workhouse, Madhouse, Gaol and Gibbet. He showed advertisements displaying the attractions at Drury Lane, including *The Road to Ruin*, while members were wanted 'to complete a Burial Society'. Of particular interest is the décor shown by Cruikshank within the 'Gin-Shops'. Casks have become coffins containing 'Old Tom', 'Blue Ruin', 'Gin and Bitters', and 'Deady's Cordial'; the bar is little more than a counter; and the floor is wooden. The beginnings of some exuberant display are, however, in evidence: the 'marbled' wooden pilasters with debased Corinthian capitals; the bunches of grapes in swags; and the ornate candelabrum (plate 36).

Later, in the series *The Drunkard's Children*, he recorded what must have been a fairly typical Gin Palace of the 1830s and 1840s. While the disastrous effects of the gin habit are clearly shown in terms of degradation, poverty, disease and madness, the drawing is of great interest architecturally. The double doors contain etched glass, and gas-light illuminates the plate-glass window. A large advertisement in florid letters, probably etched into a mirror, offers the supply of wines and spirits to families. Huge casks carried on a stand contain 'Cream of the Valley' and 'The Celebrated Double Gin'. The only capital visible is a free invention on the grape motif, and owes little to classical precedent. The bar is no longer a shop-counter, but is a fully developed pub bar-counter, in a form that has remained relatively unchanged until recent times. The illumination is bright, and is by gas. The floor is wooden, but the beginnings of grandeur and display are clearly in evidence (plate 37).

A witness reporting to a select committee of the House of Commons in 1834 contrasted the 'low, dirty public house' that had previously stood opposite his residence with the 'splendid edifice, the front ornamental with pilasters, supporting a handsome cornice and entablature and balustrades' that was the new Gin Palace. Thousands of pounds were spent in order to provide gilded columns, mahogany fronts, silver bar-engines, mirrors, and carvings of all description. The blaze of gas-light within and without a Gin Palace must have been a welcome sight to the inhabitants of the dismal half-world of the back streets. The Gin Palaces provided a refuge from dirt, failure, squalor, and hunger, and gave warmth, brightness, glamour, and company. The lushness of the décor and the exotic flash of silvered mirrors reflecting the gas-light gave the poor the fleeting illusion of finery that was never to be theirs.

The Gin Palace owners became wealthy, and the investment in first-class materials paid off as people deserted the gloomy, sordid pubs for the splendid emporia where alcohol was served by coquettes dressed in the latest modes. It was naturally important to suggest the richness of the interiors in the architectural treatment of the façades. Indeed, the great hanging gas-lights outside Victorian urban pubs identified them, and were derived from the early Gin Palaces or Temples of the 1830s.

The Victorian pub, as a field for study, is rich in lessons. It possesses the virtues of providing a series of planes upon which the traditional sign-writer can practise his art; of being an example of functional architecture at its very best in every sense; and of being a work of art where every detail is a joy.

John Grubb Richardson had pioneered in the provision of houses for his workers at Bessbrook, Newry, in 1846.[4] His namesake, B. W. Richardson, suggested many new materials such as *Lincrusta*, glazed tiles, and glazed bricks for his Utopian town of Hygeia. It is fascinating to see how these reforming and anti-pub Victorians enthused about materials which were used with enormous gusto by pub designers. *Lincrusta* was the almost universal ceiling covering, and many walls above dado level had it too. Its advantage was that it could be washed down easily, and was obtainable in many patterns.

As new techniques and material came on the market, wooden floors, 'marbled' columns and pilasters, and timber bar-counters were replaced by tiled floors, cast-iron columns, applied-colour glazed tiles for walls, and marble bar-tops. More durable and easily cleaned, these hard, robust materials gave a new richness to the Gin Palace, and, as plate-glass and mirrors became larger and more ornate, even more elaboration was possible. Even better, from the commercial point of view, was the fact that redecoration at frequent intervals was no longer necessary.

The Crown Liquor Saloon in Belfast is perhaps the best surviving example of this phase in Gin Palace design remaining in the British Isles. From the ground to the first-floor level, the structural elements of the front are expressed and entirely encrusted with a veritable orgy of coloured glazed tiles, while painted glass, a gilt and lettered fascia and a stuccoed superstructure of singular coarseness complete the picture. Inside, however, the startling richness of lettered advertisements, mirrors, a tiled long bar with a marble counter-top, painted and etched glass and fine woods give us some idea of what the true Gin Palace was like (plate 38). Yet *The Crown* survived probably because it was archaic for its date, some forty years after the first Gin Palace in London, for by then the large central horseshoe bar with radiating compartments was tending to replace the long-bar type of plan that had been usual in the early days. However, the qualities of decoration and utility found in *The Crown* were typical of the 1860s. The mirrors had practical advantages in that dark corners of the pub could be watched by staff, and small spaces could seem to be bigger.

The entrance doors of *The Crown Liquor Saloon* possess splendidly robust door-furniture with pull-handles, push-bars, and engraved plates, and the painted glass is as fine as is anywhere to be found (plate 39). The woodwork was grained or varnished for its extra hard-wearing qualities, and all fittings are larger than life to stand up to rough usage. The designer of *The Crown Liquor Saloon* was a Mr Flanagan, the son of the proprietor of the pub, who obtained from Dublin the Italian craftsmen to transform his fantasy into reality. The tiling, glasswork, carving and general workmanship are of such a high order that it is not surprising to learn that the usual employment given to the Italians was on ecclesiastical buildings. Significantly, the latter half of the nineteenth century, post-Catholic Emancipation, saw an enormous upsurge of building for the Roman Catholic Church. Workers were imported from Italy to carry out the necessary crafts usual in church work of the period, and so a considerable supply of craftsmen was then available for other work.

The detail inside *The Crown* is magnificent. Boxes or snugs are elaborately decorated with painted glass panels, carvings, tiles and mirrors. The floor is a masterpiece of the tiler's art, and the ceiling, bar, display-case, and mirrors combine in a splendid expression of High Victorian functional pub design. Yet it is unique to Belfast. There are magnificent pubs of a similar period in London, Liverpool, Dublin and other cities, but *The Crown* has a character and homogeneity all its own.

A good functional tradition of pub design had culminated in the classical extravagance of *The Crown*, but there were other even more curious products of the Victorian age. In Cromac Square, Belfast, was a corner pub that appeared to be built in the rich classical tradition with fine, bold lettering, etched glass and stucco panels, but inside possessed Gothic details in the bar-dividers and the display-stand (plate 40). The Gothic Revival came to Belfast late and, apart from the delightful romanticism of the Deaf and Dumb Institute (demolished) and Queen's College, both by Lanyon, and the Carlisle Memorial Church Group, produced little of greatness. Bad Gothic was rampant by the 1870s, however, and many Belfast pubs echo this in their interior décor, but save for half-a-dozen spectacular examples, mostly destroyed, the Gothic influence on pub design must be seen as essentially fleeting and of interest only as a curiosity.

In the last two decades of Victoria's reign, the urban pub was becoming truly palatial. A corner site was considered important to attract as many customers as possible, and the original ideas of ornate pilasters, plate-glass, and large hanging gas-lamps were carried to their logical conclusion. Plate-glass windows became vast, and displayed numbers of gas-lights instead of the one or two flares usual in the earlier period. There were several entrances rather than one or two, and these gave access to separate rooms grouped around a central island-bar, thus ensuring that the maximum number of persons and tastes were catered for with a minimum number of staff.

The rooms of the later pubs were divided by screens, containing etched glass panels. Often, 'snob-screens' were provided at the bar containing panels that swivelled on their vertical axes, and these protected the users of the saloon or private bars from the gaze of the vulgar using the 'public'. The swivelling panels also enabled drinkers to order without being seen by anyone in other bars, and they were used in Gin Palaces from 1860 onwards.

The display-fitment of the late Gin Palace was derived from the early showing of casks and bottles as depicted by Cruikshank. Eventually it became a massive fantasy of mirrors, casks, bottles, glasses and mahogany, and was either placed at the back of the bar or on an island site in the centre of the U-shaped or central bar. Beer-engines had handles of porcelain or wood, and advertisements had that uninhibited zest so disliked by the disciples of 'Good Taste' in the 1920s and 1930s.

The Gin Palace, which developed into the late-Victorian and Edwardian urban pub, was a great nineteenth-century invention, yet it was only an exaggeration and concentration of all the familiar items necessary for the functioning of a pub. Casks, bottles, bars, and glasses were put on view, mirrored, and set within a rich décor that was theatrical and brash, but eminently suitable for its purpose. If we examine our city pubs today, we shall find fragments of a tradition that started in the 1830s, but practically nowhere is there a Gin Palace that has survived intact. Nevertheless, as functional design, the Gin Palace has much to teach us today.[5]

Notes to this chapter are on page 118

CHAPTER 7

Prisons and Hospitals

Come, let's away to prison.
William Shakespeare, *King Lear*

The planning of prisons and hospitals followed similar lines during the late eighteenth century. 'Not only were the two kinds of buildings intended to foster the improvement of their occupants, either morally or physically, but their functions also tended to overlap.'[1] Obviously the problems of providing for the sick in the larger towns created new difficulties which had to be solved. Although octagonal plans had been produced for prisons, and provided the inspiration behind the *Panopticon* of Bentham, and although Soane, Elmes and others had designed geometrical plans, the practical Victorians appear to have favoured regular blocks separated by courts or by open spaces.

The primary influence in the improvement of prison conditions was John Howard, whose *The State of Prisons in England and Wales* (1777) proved of lasting benefit. Hygiene and straightforward functional planning were among Howard's main concerns, themes to which he returned in *Lazarettos* (1789).[2, 3]

Among the practical men influenced by Howard's ideas was Sir Edmund Frederick Du Cane (1830-1903), like so many distinguished Victorians an officer in the Royal Engineers. He rose to the rank of Major-General, and his work covers a very remarkable range of activities.

Du Cane was assistant superintendent of the foreign side of the Great Exhibition of 1851 and gained considerable experience of organisation and constructional problems during this time. From 1851 to 1856 he organised convict labour in Western Australia, and used his understanding of building technique in order to promote public works and improvements.

He was recalled by the outbreak of the Crimean War, and joined for duty at the War Office under the Inspector-General of Fortifications in August 1856. He was employed on designs and estimates for new defences proposed for dockyards and naval bases, but in 1863 was appointed Director of Convict Prisons and Inspector of Military Prisons. When transportation was abolished in 1867, he was responsible for the provision of the vast amount of additional prison accommodation necessary, and in 1869 he succeeded Sir Edmund Henderson as Chairman of the Board of Directors of Convict Prisons, Surveyor-General of Prisons, and Inspector-General of Military Prisons. He reorganised the County and Borough Prisons, and was a driving a force behind the Prison Act of 1877, which was a major Victorian enactment. Du Cane encouraged the use of fingerprints in the detection of crime.

He designed many of the Victorian landmarks at Dover, and the chain of land forts at Plymouth between 1858 and 1863. His publications on fortifications are of considerable interest, and I reproduce two plates from his Papers on Fortifications in Iron (1862) (figs 4 and 5). These were very advanced for their date, and it is interesting that even as late as the 1860s and 1870s so much thought was given to the design of forts of iron, for only half a century later the Dreadnoughts

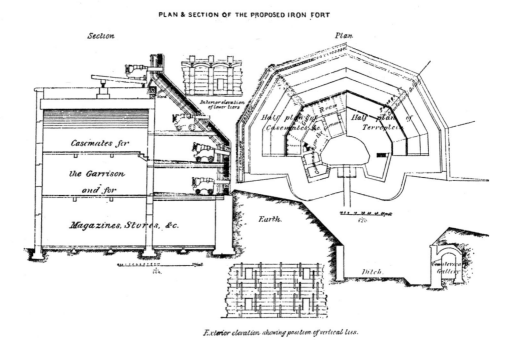

PLAN & SECTION OF THE PROPOSED IRON FORT

Section   Plan.

Exterior elevation showing position of vertical ties.

Fig 4 *Details of an iron fort from* Papers on Fortification in Iron *by Sir Edmund Du Cane, published in 1862. The shape of the plan owes something to Renaissance examples of fortification, but the use of the 'modern' material, iron, is of great interest, especially when we consider that the design is just over a century old*

and mighty guns were to render forts obsolete. I have, through the kindness of his direct descendant, Mr A. W. Pullan, examined Sir Edmund's papers. Among writings relevant to this book are his manuscripts on 'Mechanics, Machinery, and Metallurgy', which contain a charming drawing of a steam-engine by Hero of Alexandria of *c*.120 BC. There is also a fascinating paper on 'Balance Musket-Proof Shutters for Embrasures, Windows, &c' and notes on the 'Jarrah Timber of Western Australia, which is proof against the White Ant and Sea Worm', presumably dating from his 1851-6 spell as an organiser of convict labour. There are many papers on prison labour, punishment, hygiene and all manner of topics relevant to the penal system. Sir Edmund was the originator of a comprehensive scheme for the transfer to the Government of all local prisons and the whole cost of their maintenance.

Du Cane's monument, as far as this book is concerned, is his great work, Wormwood Scrubs Prison. This was built to replace a prison at Millbank, the site of which had become very valuable. The site of Wormwood Scrubs was

SUNKEN TOWER WITH IRON PARAPETS.

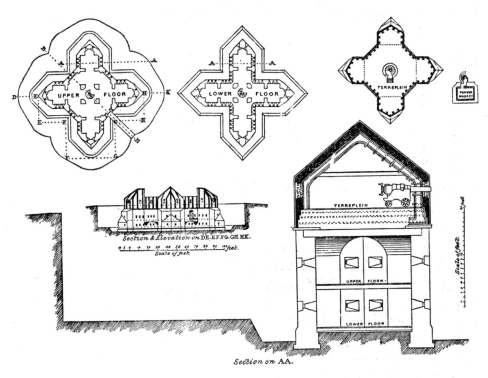

Section & Elevation on DE.EF.FG.GH.HK.
Scale of feet.

Section on AA.

Fig 5 *Sunken Tower with Iron Parapets from* Papers on Fortification in Iron *by Sir Edmund Du Cane, published in 1862. This fortress could well have sprung from the mind of a Renaissance military engineer, but for the extensive use of iron plates. The design is a fascinating survival of Victorian attitudes to defence*

obtained from the Ecclesiastical Commissioners, and the whole building was erected by convict labour, on lines of organisation developed from Du Cane's Australian days. Bricks were made on site, the boundary wall was completed in 1883, and there were cells for 1,381 convicts, with a cookhouse, bakery, laundry, workshops, chapel and baths. Cell blocks were built parallel to each other, orientated north-south, and each block contained 351 cells. Blocks were joined by covered ways (fig 6).

The prison is remarkable for its clean, logical plans and the heating and air-conditioning system which fed each cell (figs 7 and 8). Staircases, vents and sanitary stacks were expressed in the building, and the completed prison combines that direct integrity familiar from early warehouse and industrial buildings with a mildly Romanesque concession to fenestration and detail (plate 44).

F

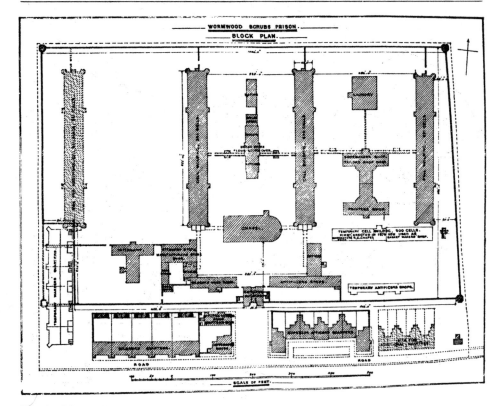

Fig 6 *Plan of Wormwood Scrubs Prison, showing temporary buildings erected during the building of the permanent structure. The whole building was erected using convict labour on lines of organisation developed from Du Cane's days in Australia. Even the bricks were made on site*

Du Cane supervised the building of Wormwood Scrubs himself, charging a guinea a day, pointing out in a letter of 30 August 1873 that by employing convict labour and supervising it himself he was avoiding architects' and surveyors' fees, and therefore saving public money. His methods caused unease among many, and he got into hot water with the Secretary of State for expressing his views in print (10 April 1894). He was attacked as an autocrat in *The Daily Chronicle* of 23 January 1894; but simple, functional, cheap solutions devised by men of vision are always attacked by those who prefer bureaucracy, chronic wastage of public money, and complicated bumbledom.

Du Cane, a great Victorian functionalist, died on 7 July 1903 at 10 Portman Square. He was buried in the churchyard of Great Braxted in Essex.[4]

The separate blocks of prison design were also employed in hospitals to avoid the spread of infection and to enable light and air to penetrate the blocks ade-

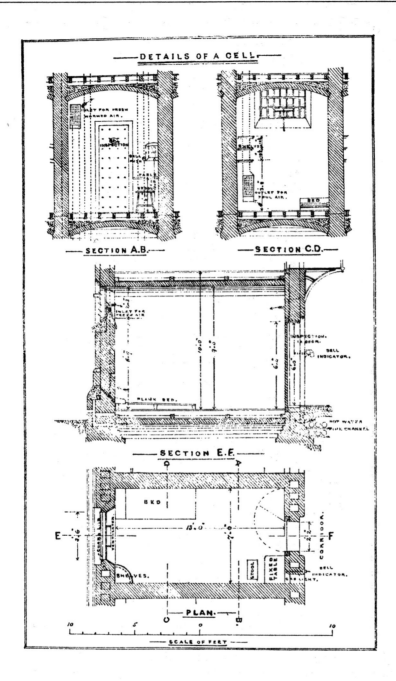

Fig 7 *Detail of a cell in Wormwood Scrubs Prison. Great attention was paid to ventilation and heating, and the general robust quality of the structure deserves notice*

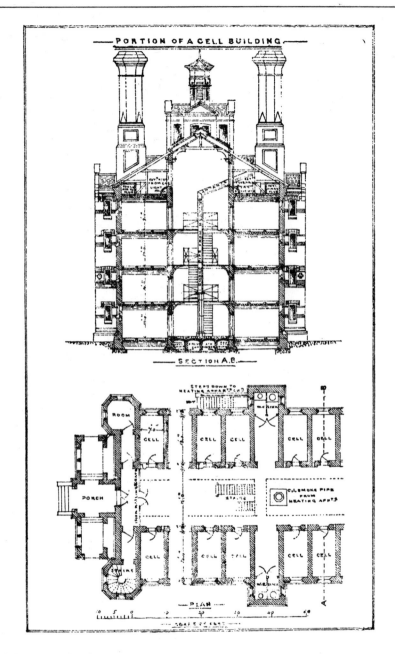

Fig 8 *Section and plan of part of a cell block in Wormwood Scrubs Prison. The arrangement of central galleries and the vertical stacks for services is noteworthy, economical, and logical. The provision of gas-light made attention to ventilation essential*

quately. The scientific study of infection really began in the eighteenth century, and was reflected in proposals for hospitals. J. R. Tenon, in his *Mémoires sur les hôpitaux de Paris* (Paris 1788), suggested that the 'pavilion' type of design was most suitable for hospitals, and quoted the Royal Naval Hospital near Plymouth as an ideal type of plan.[5] This hospital was also specifically mentioned by Howard.[6]

Perhaps the most spectacular of all 'pavilion' hospitals was the new St Thomas's, built between Westminster Bridge and Lambeth Palace, and completed in 1870-1. Some nine acres of land known as Stangate Bank were purchased from the Board of Works at a cost of about £100,000, and the existing tenements, wharves and boathouses were demolished. The foreshore was reclaimed, and this accounted for about half of the site.

The hospital was built as eight pavilions linked by corridors. The central six buildings were for patients; that next to Westminster Bridge was for officers of the hospital; and that to the south was the school of medicine, with a museum and lecture-room (plates 42 and 43).

The foundations presented certain difficulties, and towards the river front some twenty-eight feet had to be excavated before firm clay was reached. A solid base of concrete was laid, and on this the pavilions were built. The whole structure was fire-resistant, the floors of each storey being laid on iron girders protected by concrete. Floor finishes of oak ensured a good appearance and hardwearing qualities, while the walls of each ward were coated with Parian cement. Heating was augmented by a warm-water system, and natural ventilation was encouraged by open fires. A contemporary opinion of the hospital was that 'the plan . . . may be considered perfect; and although it cost in all at least half a million of money, it is a cheap outlay for the good it is certain to effect for ages to come. As an addition to the great public edifices of the metropolis, it certainly will not be surpassed in appearance . . .'[7] A comparison with the new buildings now (1972) is sufficient to emphasise the accuracy of the latter statement.

The architect of St Thomas's Hospital was Henry Currey, a competent designer in the Italianate manner favoured during the 1860s and 1870s. The design of St Thomas's is adapted from that of the hospital at Lariboisère, and was influenced by the opinions of Florence Nightingale. Associated with this great scheme was the construction of the Albert Embankment under the direction of Sir Joseph Bazalgette for the Metropolitan Board of Works.

The pavilion approach to hospital design was generally accepted as a functional solution to the problem during Victoria's reign. One of the specialists in the planning of hospitals was Saxon Snell, who designed the astonishing St Charles Hospital in North Kensington, London. This architect, who practised with his sons Henry Saxon Snell and Alfred Saxon Snell at 22 Southampton Buildings,

WC, was a member of the Architectural Association in 1850, and was one of its oldest members. His career was very much involved in the harnessing of new inventions to serve functional buildings. His work concerning the design of hospitals enabled him to write *Charitable and Parochial Institutions* and, with Dr F. J. Mouatt, *Hospital Construction and Management*. He was an assistant of Sir Joseph Paxton and of Sir William Tite. He was the chief draughtsman in the Science and Art Department, South Kensington, and assisted Captain Fowke in the Dublin Exhibition and the 1861 Exhibition. In 1851 he won the RA Silver Medal for measured drawings of St Mary-le-Bow. In 1866 he was appointed architect to the St Marylebone Board of Guardians. He died in his seventy-third year in Putney. A week before his death he was much occupied 'with his scheme for solving the problem of hospital sites in London by building in the public parks'.[8]

The foundation-stone of what was the new infirmary for the sick poor of the parish of St Marylebone was laid in 1879 by Edmund Boulnois, the chairman of the Board of Guardians. The site, of 3½ acres, is near Ladbroke Grove,

> and is a parallelogram in shape, with its longest sides having frontages to Rackham-street and Treverton-street. The building is being erected by the Guardians, in pursuance of the provisions of the Metropolitan Poor Act, 1867, and under the orders of the local Government Board. It will contain accommodation for the care and treatment of 760 of the sick poor of the parish. The architects are Messrs Saxon Snell and Son. A contract has been entered into with Messrs Wall Bros for the erection of the building, with all its fittings and engineering works, for 109,000 *l*., and it is estimated that the total cost, including the price paid for the land and the furniture and fittings, will be at the rate of about 160 *l*. per bed.[9]

The general arrangement consisted of a block of buildings 'situated at the entrance' containing the residences of the medical officer, matron and assistant medical officer; and over the arched carriage-way in the centre there was a chapel with accommodation for 180 people. The architects provided a description of the buildings, later published by Batsford, in which much was made of the function of the building, including the efficiency of air changes, the system of natural ventilation and the heating. The latter was by open fires which heated coils of pipes containing water which then circulated. Humidity was also controlled so that air would not be dried, a great advance for the time. The lighting was by gas, and fumes were carefully vented away.[10]

The system of linked pavilion-blocks which Snell devised was very forward-looking. The administration block was in the centre, flanked on either side by two double-ward blocks parallel to each other and to the central block, so that, including the central or administration block, the main buildings consisted of five blocks parallel to each other.

The buildings are planned on what is now well known as the pavilion principle, so that each block of buildings is, as far as is compatible with facility
of communication and administration, isolated from other portions of the
building. The entrance is in Rackham Street, on the south side of the site,
through a spacious gateway, over which is the chapel, 60ft long by 30ft
wide, with boarded wagon-roof of trefoil section, 22ft high to the wall-plate,
and about 45ft to apex. Sittings are provided for 250 persons. The interior
walls and tracery of the windows are very nicely executed in white Suffolk
bricks. The chapel is warmed by means of one of Mr. Saxon Snell's patent
'Thermhydric' stoves ... Flanking the entrance gateway and chapel are
residences for the medical officers ...[11]

The 'Thermhydric' system allowed for upright flues in the external walls.
Inlets were provided for fresh air, which was warmed as it entered, and air was
also admitted directly through the walls, into skirting-boxes between the beds.
The flues carried off the foul air and the products of gas combustion. The building incorporated a logical, functional system of services.

The central feature of the administration block is a massive tower, 182ft
high, which forms a landmark as seen from the north and west. Inside this tower
the chimney shaft from the boilers below is carried up. The upper part of the
tower, very northern-Italian in inspiration, contains a number of large tanks,
affording storage for 25,000gal of water. A well, sunk on the site 500ft deep, and
powerful pumps provided water at the rate of 6,000gal per hour.[12]

The pavilions grouped round this tower are linked to each other by light cast-
iron galleries and canopied ways which join the brickwork with an admirable
candour and a satisfying resolution. The excellent brickwork, strong self-confident
design, and assured functional planning and detail make the St Charles Hospital
one of the most interesting and forward-looking buildings in Kensington (plate
45). It was opened by their Royal Highnesses the Prince and Princess of Wales
on 29 June 1881. The contracts for the whole, including services, totalled
£113,000, or £150 per bed.[13]

The principles of design explained in this chapter remained the basis for
hospital and prison design throughout the nineteenth century, and indeed into
the twentieth. The larger hospitals built during World War II for the Services
owe their planning to eighteenth-century prototypes, while advances in func-

tional design were directly derived from the great pragmatic schemes of the Victorian designers.[14]

Notes to this chapter are on pages 118-19

CHAPTER 8

The Search for Durable Materials and Healthier Cities

Ah, to build, to build !
That is the noblest art of all the arts.
Painting and sculpture are but images,
Are merely shadows cast by outward things
On stone or canvas, having in themselves
No separate existence. Architecture,
Existing in itself, and not in seeming
A something it is not, surpasses them
As substance shadow.
        Longfellow, *Michael Angelo*, part 1, sec 2

In order to understand how improvements in architecture and environmental technology came about in Victorian times, we must try to imagine the fashionable legacy of Nash and his followers. It will be recalled that Suetonius observed in *Divus Augustus* that the Emperor boasted he had found Rome brick and left it marble (*urbem . . . excoluit adeo, ut iure sit gloriatus marmoream se relinquere, quam latericiam accepisset*). It was said of John Nash that he found London brick and left it plaster.

It must be remembered that when George IV moved to a transformed Buckingham Palace, polite society moved to the environs of the Court. Regency London was the model for stucco-faced Belgravia and later developments in Kensington, Paddington, and Chelsea. The unified stucco façades with Italianate detailing and classical porticoes became the standard treatment of housing for the well-to-do. It was unfortunate that use of that architectural style should coincide with a population explosion in London, and with the coming of the railways and gas-light.

Air pollution was a conspicuous evil of Victorian London, and stucco was ill-adapted to the corrosive effects of London fog. Early Victorian stucco was not painted gleaming and white as we see it today, but was, in fact, coloured to look like stone, and was satisfactory in Regency times when the problem of air pollution was not great. When, however, the numbers of coal-fires increased, the railways came, gas-light was introduced, and coal-fired power invaded the industrial areas, rapid deterioration of stucco due to atmosphere pollution was to be expected. Fashion decreed that the Italianate style should continue to be used, with the result that oil paint had to be applied to stucco to preserve it, an expensive and hardly satisfactory state of affairs.

Even when stucco was used sparingly, as in the charming houses on the Lloyd-Baker estate in Clerkenwell, designed by John and William Joseph Booth in 1819[1] (plate 46), the problems of maintenance became acute.

The dense population living in the new industrialised society created environmental problems of waste-disposal, disease, water-supply and the marketing of food. Great covered markets were built, including Billingsgate, Smithfield and the Leadenhall Market (plate 41). Factory Acts and other legislation improving sanitary and ventilating techniques had to be passed, while all the resources of Victorian inventiveness were called upon to solve the difficulties of providing adequate artificial lighting, ventilation and warmth. It is interesting to note that the design of iron and brass bedsteads, which to later generations appeared over-elaborate, had a functional origin. The main supports of the bed had bulbous bases over castors to discourage bed-bugs from climbing up to torment the sleeper. The wheels of beds were often placed in small cups of camphor or paraffin as a further deterrent to these ferocious pests. The iron straps that supported the mattress could not harbour vermin, and were also a functional advance. It is forgotten today how common were lice, bugs and fleas in Victorian times.

The pollution of the air in cities by the waste products of industry and power-generation created tremendous problems in terms of both health and architectural design. Bad health among workers was a problem not only on humanitarian grounds but also in terms of loss of working capacity. Clearly, labourers with poor lungs were not as efficient as healthy lads from the unpolluted countryside. It is difficult for us to imagine what Victorian London was like when the frequent fogs fouled faces, clothes, lungs, and buildings. Atmospheric pollution was a killer, and conditions in Manchester, Liverpool and London were at times absolutely intolerable. Concern for proper ventilation in an age of gas-light was voiced by the medical profession, and early attempts to provide it have already been mentioned. Ernest Jacob noted that clergymen often had headaches on Mondays following Sundays spent in overcrowded, badly ventilated churches.[2]

Butterfield and others attempted to solve the problem of church interiors becoming dulled and dirty by the introduction of glazed tiles and brickwork. Gin palaces were provided with marble, tiles, glass, and mirrors for easy cleaning. Similar movements took place in domestic design, and the work of Halsey Ricardo is of singular interest, since not only did he formulate his own philosophy of materials, but he analysed the revolt against tradition in favour of function.

In his lecture, 'Of Colour in the Architecture of Cities',[3] Ricardo noted that the revolt

> against the grey stucco-fronted houses was in part due to the same feeling that followed on the Gothic Revival—a desire to avoid anything that might savour of dishonesty in construction, but the red buildings arose more, I think, as a protest against the monotony and colourlessness of our streets. Now that we have tasted blood—so to speak—we want more, and we want it permanent. Red brick and terra-cotta discolour; coloured stones and marbles grow dim and perish in shocking haste; and it would seem as if no building material but what had got practically a glass face to it would be able to contend against the corrosion of the air of a manufacturing town.[4]

Ricardo argued that the use of coloured materials would supply the equivalents of the shadows and half-tones provided traditionally by cornices, pilasters, and mouldings. The 'red buildings' were, of course, the houses designed by Philip Webb, Norman Shaw and others in a reaction against stucco Italianate domestic design.

Ricardo urged that 'want and disease, dirt and disorder' should be fought against, and urged: 'strong and brave, let us go out to our fight clothed with

the distinction that colour can give us, and cheered by the *camaraderie* that such
colour confers : and, the day's work done, there is the city beautiful—firm, stable,
our home.'[5] These are brave words, but his philosophy was to be expounded
further in his justification of the houses he built in Melbury Road, Kensington.

> An endeavour has been made in building these houses, to recognise and
> accept the present conditions of house-building in London—more especially
> as regards the dirt and the impurities of the atmosphere. They are faced
> externally throughout with salt-glazed bricks, which, being of fire-clay
> vitrified at a high temperature, may be looked upon as proof against the
> disintegrating forces of the London air. These bricks being virtually un-
> changeable, I have had to renounce the aid that time gives to a building by
> blunting its edges, softening and blending its colours : but as a *per contra*
> one has the satisfaction of knowing that the house is built of durable
> materials, wind-proof and rain-proof : and whatever effect one can manage
> to secure, that effect is indestructible. In the case of the usual brick house
> —whilst the brick and stone are ageing and weathering, the woodwork is
> periodically being renewed (in effect) by repainting—and the acquired
> harmony of the whole is constantly being dislocated by this renewal : but
> with these houses, every time the external woodwork is recoloured the
> bricks can be washed down and the original effect—for what it is worth—
> maintained. The halls, passages, staircases, bath-rooms, etc, have their walls
> covered with tiles and their floors laid with marble. No baths, pipes, or
> sanitary fittings have casings.[6]

These observations relate to Nos 55-7 Melbury Road, Kensington.[7] Near by, in
Addison Road, Ricardo also designed a house for Sir Ernest Debenham, and his
philosophy of using hard, impervious materials to clothe the exterior is again in
evidence. Large numbers of William de Morgan tiles were used to decorate the
interior.

It is not too far a jump from Halsey Ricardo, gin-palace finishes, or some of
the other functional ideas and buildings mentioned to an expression of Victorian
functionalism at its most obvious. Salt-glazed bricks, tiles, terrazzo, and other
hard, washable materials were ideally suited to the underground public convenience found in so many Victorian cities (plate 48).

Not unconnected with such conveniences were vast and far-reaching reforms
largely introduced by Edwin Chadwick, Secretary to the Poor Law Commissioners. Outbreaks of typhoid and cholera caused deaths on a very large scale and
created crises in public health. A report by the Poor Law Commissioners in 1838
on epidemics in Whitechapel led to Chadwick's *Report on the Sanitary Con-*

ditions of the Labouring Population of 1842. Although the Medical Establishment maintained that cholera was caused by fogs, cucumbers, or 'miasma', among other improbable scapegoats, Chadwick, a lawyer, believed that the key lay in the water supply, and its contamination by sewage. Later, in the 1850s, it was proved that cholera was carried in drinking water that had been polluted by human excreta. This lent great support to Chadwick's ideas, and he was able to declare that three things were absolutely necessary in the growing towns and cities: piped, pure water; a system of sewers; and the safe disposal of the sewage. In order to provide these benefits, towns would have to construct, operate, and maintain the systems; be empowered to compel house-owners to use them; and levy rates to cover costs of construction and operation.[8, 9] Before 1817 most drinking water was carried in wooden or lead pipes which could not withstand great pressures, so leakages and pollution were common. Cast iron came into general use after 1817 for water-supply pipes. Although Harington had invented water-closets in late Elizabethan times, they did not come into general use until the late eighteenth century, and were usually found in basements or on the first floor. Closets on upper floors had to have the water pumped up to the cisterns by hand-pumps, as the pressure of the mains was very low. Only in Victorian times, when cast-iron pipes and steam-engines assisted the increase in water-pressure, could water-supply be guaranteed to feed upper floors.

Advances in the filtration of water to remove solids were made by James Simpson in 1829, and legislation was pressed so that by 1856 all water companies had installed filtration plants, and took their supplies from the Thames above the polluted, tidal reaches.[10]

It was Sir Joseph Bazalgette who created the great system that solved the problem of sewage collection and disposal in London. He designed a great pattern of sewers leading east, intercepted by a secondary system of sewers laid along both banks of the river, eventually discharging into settlement tanks at the northern and southern outfalls from which the effluent could be pumped out after high water. Bazalgette's scheme was enormous in its conception, and involved the construction of nearly 1,500 miles of sewers, the building of the Thames Embankment, and the erection of pumping-stations. At the Lambeth factory of Doulton, stoneware pipes were manufactured which were both strong and impervious. The use of Portland cement to bond the brickwork in the sewers was another innovation introduced by Bazalgette, and the tests carried out during the construction of the sewers from 1859 to 1866 enabled cement manufacturers to improve their products.[11]

Two of Bazalgette's pumping-stations deserve special mention: those at Crossness and Abbey Mills, the former because it still contains the beam-engines, and the latter because of the superb architectural detail. The style chosen for the architecture was said by *The Builder* to be 'Mediaeval with Byzantine and Norman features', while the buildings had 'an amount of decoration in carved stone to doorways and other parts, that may be deemed great . . .'. James Watt & Co provided the engines, which were placed symmetrically within marvellous interiors of polychrome brickwork. The various galleries and levels are carried on robust iron columns with foliate capitals (plate 49). Light filters down from a central octagonal cupola, illuminating wonderful cast-iron detail. Even the floors of the cat-walks are composed of beautifully cast geometrical patterns (plate 50), and the balustrades are exquisite examples of High Victorian design (plate 51). Note how the baluster is bolted onto the beam, and how the support-castings are bolted simply to the baluster and the handrails. The way in which the panels of cast iron forming the floor are simply laid should also be noted. The beautiful door-hinges, of naturalistic pattern, support enormous doors, and give added strength to the panels (plate 52). The exterior of Abbey Mills pumping-station has a cathedralesque quality, and the Byzantine cupola adds greatly to the illusion that the building is an Orthodox Church. The base of one of the former chimneys, regrettably demolished, may be seen.

The remarkable Bazalgette was a pupil of McNeill, one of Telford's assistants. His achievement was not only a major triumph of engineering: it was a victory over death, disease and squalor; and aesthetically it was a masterpiece. The sewers themselves are beautiful in their grand simplicity, with something of the quality of Roman structures, and the pumping-stations are functional, logical, and architecturally very successful.[12]

Indeed, the Victorian pumping-station became the subject of elaborate architectural treatment not confined to the building itself, but extended to the engines and castings.

It is hardly surprising that pumping-stations should have been treated in this way, for by the 1860s it was an accepted tenet of architectural theory that not only should a building work, but that concepts such as social reform, mass-education, and the uplifting example of architectural excellence should be remembered in their creation. The similarity of Abbey Mills to a Greek Orthodox cathedral is not so bizarre as at first it may appear. The cleaning-up of great cities, the improving of public health, and the saving of life had a moral as well as practical side, so something of the magnificence of a religious building may be found in sewage pumping-stations.

The greatest exponent of the theory of the architecture of meaning was undoubtedly John Claudius Loudon, whose *Encyclopaedia of Cottage, Farm and Villa Architecture* sets out his views. Loudon's theory of architecture was strongly moral, as might be expected of a Scot, but it was tempered by the common-sense philosophy derived from Hume and others. Loudon exalted the taste of the common man, and demanded social reform, wholesale education and the improvement of minds. In the context of art, beauty was in the eye of the beholder, who determines whether something is acceptable or not. To Loudon and men like him, the purpose of education was to give to the minds of men, all men, as many potential associations as possible, so that the purpose of the artist was to strike an answering chord in the educated man by creating an association in his mind. Archibald Alison wrote that, if we saw a building, it might be beautiful to us, but that, if we knew it was the residence of any person whose memory we admire,

> a train of associations comes to mind. The delight with which we recollect the traces of their lives, blends itself insensibly with the emotions which the scenery excites; and the admiration which these recollections afford, seems to give a kind of sanctity to the place where they dwelt, and converts everything into beauty which appears to have been connected with them.[13]

Styles, for Loudon, were ephemeral, but had temporary functions in that they could awaken untutored minds to a sense of history. As universal education progressed, so, to Loudon, the necessity for 'styles' as such would cease to be important. His illustrations in the *Encyclopaedia* shows his versatility from Cardboard Gothick to the 'Indian' style of Nash; but his insistence on fitness for function anticipates the Victorian architecture of railway-stations, pumping-stations, glass-houses, and domestic design.

Loudon insisted that chimneys, windows and doors expressed the facts of the plan of a building as well as its function, and attempted to apply Alison's principles to a theory of architecture. The expression of architectural style was less important to Loudon than fitness or use.[14] Turrets could express 'commodiousness and convenience; it being supposed that their object, in modern houses, is to supply closets . . .'.[15] Verandahs, balconies, and colonnades expressed comfort and elegance, although these may exist in plain, unarticulated buildings. There could never be beauty, however, Loudon insisted, until the truths of a building were expressed by the massing, materials and openings.[16] Thus the formal effects of Victorian picturesque architecture, according to Loudon, were in essence expressive of function. 'Fitness for the end in view' was Loudon's creed, and he abhorred fakery and pretence. 'The beauty of truth is so essential to every other kind of beauty, that it can neither be dispensed with in art nor in morals.'[17] Of course, in the design of farm buildings, Loudon insisted that there was a great range of functional expression, and that the purpose of each building should be at once discernible to the discriminating eye.[18]

Yet of all the claimants to innovation of glass-house construction, the first must be John Claudius Loudon, who revolutionised the design of conservatories by the invention of an iron ridge and furrow structure, with wrought-iron sash-bars that could be easily bent. It was Loudon, in fact, who first made curvilinear glazed roofs possible. Prototypes of his invention were presented to the Horticultural Society in 1816, and subsequently illustrated in his *An Encyclopaedia of Gardening* published in 1822. He erected his first experimental glass-house in the grounds of his house in Porchester Terrace, Bayswater, and published *A Comparative View of the Common and Curvilinear Modes of roofing Hothouses*, with a description of the various uses to which his invention could be put, in 1818, and followed this with *Sketches of Curvilinear Hothouses, with a description of the various Purposes in Horticultural and General Architecture, to which a Solid Iron Sash Bar (lately invented) is Applicable*. The hothouses erected by Loudon pre-date Paxton's work, and showed both Turner and Burton the way (plate 53). Probably the most spectacular of all early glass-houses was the conservatory designed for Mrs Beaumont in 1827 at Bretton Hall in Yorkshire, using the Loudon method of construction. It was illustrated in *An Encyclopaedia of Cottage, Farm, and Villa Architecture, and Furniture*, published in 1833. The fact that Loudon disposed of his rights in his invention to W. and D. Bailey of Holborn in 1818, and that his own financial problems drove him further into the world of pure gardening, tends to obscure his significance in the development of glass-house construction. As with so much of Victorian invention, development, and taste, Loudon is the key figure. He was the complete opposite of the reactionary Pugin, and represents the forward-looking, adventurous, truly inventive Victorian, rather than a pedantic eclectic. The immense works on gardening, architecture, management of farms and houses, pleasure grounds, hothouses, agriculture, forestry, landscape gardening, furniture, and, finally, cemeteries, reveal a breathtaking sense of expertise, aesthetic judgement, and capacity for sheer hard work. Mr John Gloag has written an admirable work on Loudon which tells the story succinctly under the title *Mr Loudon's England. The life and Work of John Claudius Loudon, and his influence on architecture and furniture design* (Newcastle-upon-Tyne, 1970). Loudon emerges as the great Victorian Practical Man, a functionalist of the first order, and a giant even for an age of Olympians. His achievements have been clouded and hidden by the later propaganda put about by the apologists for Gothic Revival, and by the cult of the Great Architect, which has boosted the Pugins, Scotts, Butterfields, and others at the expense of practical Victorians. Perhaps Loudon's enthusiasm for what might be described as the Batty Langley School of Gothic as illustrated in his *Encyclopaedia* earned him the opprobrium of the scholarly eclectics, and his association with W. H. Leeds, E. Buckton Lamb, and William Frome Smallwood produced a savage caricature in Pugin's *The True Principles of Pointed or Christian Archi-*

G

tecture of 1841. Rogue Gothicists were hardly likely to gain the approval of the Ecclesiologists, and it is perhaps as well for Loudon's reputation today that E. Bassett Keeling was much too young to contribute designs to Loudon's work. As it was, the designs displayed in the *Encyclopaedia* came in for some denunciation, and although Loudon's productions were popular, his work soon fell out of favour with the moralists and followers of Pugin, Ruskin, and others of that type.

Loudon's influence extends to that Victorian realism of function that blended with extraordinary boldness of form. The educational aspects of even a pumping-station were not overlooked and, in the consideration of the burial of the dead, Loudon observed that 'churchyards and cemeteries are scenes not only calculated to improve the morals and the taste, and by their botanical riches to cultivate the intellect, but they serve as *historical records*'.[19] There again, the origins of the Victorian cemeteries lie in the functional need to improve hygiene; but this story is told in full in my book *The Victorian Celebration of Death*.[20]

Notes to this chapter are on page 119

CHAPTER 9

A Model Town

Drink and Lust are at the
bottom of it all
                    Sir Titus Salt

When Benjamin Disraeli suggested, in his celebrated novel *Sybil*, that between employer and employee there should be a relationship more edifying than the payment and receipt of wages, he started a train of thought that was eagerly taken up by the more enlightened industrialists of an expanding, outward-going, Victorian England. Not by any means the least intelligent and humane of these entrepreneurs, Titus Salt embraced this notion and put it into effect in a practical way.

Salt was born of poor parents in 1803 but, through hard work, devotion to the principles of solid piety and the application of a great deal of imagination, he became the owner of several mills in Bradford and, indeed, became mayor of that borough in 1848. During his term of office, the problems of the poor and under-privileged were considerable, and he was the guiding light in the formation of public parks, libraries and other amenities to improve the lot of the culturally impoverished community living in appalling conditions of dirt, squalor and industrial blight. Salt was so disgusted by what he saw that he determined to do what he could to alleviate matters. Subsequent epidemics of cholera, typhoid, and other diseases brought home to thinking men that all was not well with the industrial cities, and Salt, to his undying credit, decided to do something about the causes responsible for filth and overcrowding.

The brilliant idea of using cheap alpaca fibres to make worsted cloth was to found a fortune which Salt used to create a model town outside Bradford. Experience in the courts, municipal institutions and industrial establishments had convinced him that socially and morally mid-nineteenth-century England was not all it might be. Balgarnie, in his book *Sir Titus Salt, His Life and Lessons*, published in London in 1877, states that Salt originally intended to retire at the early age of fifty in order to enjoy the life of a country squire, but decided, in view of his large family and his aversion to contributing further to the overcrowding of Bradford, to build a large manufacturing establishment with housing for the workers on a virgin site.

Salt was of the opinion that the troubles of the nation were due primarily to 'drink and lust', and he further pronounced that these two factors were 'at the bottom of it all'. Accordingly, he decided to improve the condition of his workpeople so that family life would be strengthened and other temptations, in the guise of the Demon Drink, would be rigorously excluded. In 1850 he commissioned the architects Lockwood and Mawson, of Bradford, to design a new mill at Shipley Glen, some four miles away from the town. After a visit to the new Crystal Palace in 1851, which Salt had considered buying, he decided to erect a factory on the most advanced lines, embodying the latest inventions and methods of construction, on the banks of the River Aire. In the event, the site was cleverly chosen, for, apart from its natural beauties, a railway and canal were already in being to provide suitable transport for raw materials and the finished products.

The factory, a large Italianate building, was begun, and plans were drawn up for a model town, laid out on a gridiron pattern, with ample open spaces, churches, a hospital, almshouses, schools, and a Club and Institute. Salt, though a devout Congregationalist, did not attempt to compel attendance at his own church. He granted sites to the Methodists, the Baptists, the Roman Catholics and the Swedenborgians. Religious belief of any variety was most important, in his opinion, and abstention from alcohol was essential to a godly, righteous, and useful life. Indeed, the *Saltaire Monthly Magazine* of March 1871 expressed thanks to the founder of the town 'for his stern exercise of his proprietorial rights, through which he preserved the residents . . . from the annoyance and temptation of public houses and beer shops'.

The factory was opened in 1853, a banquet being provided for two and a half thousand workers and over a thousand other guests. The Earl of Harewood, who attended the gargantuan feast (which was apparently teetotal), opined that he had developed a high notion of the manufacturing classes as a result, and the *Bradford Observer* waxed lyrical on the virtues of the new building. It is built of local stone, is six storeys high (plate 1), and the floors are of arched brick construction carried on huge cast-iron columns. The large plate-glass windows were designed to admit as much light and air as possible and the tall chimney, 250ft high, recalling an Italian campanile, was fitted with patent fuel economisers to remove 'annoying effluvium'. Indeed, 'The Works' was an up-to-date establishment for its time, and today is a noble monument to Victorian industrial functional architecture, still in working order.

Lockwood and Mawson's work is solid and well-proportioned, and their mastery of style is demonstrated in the town itself. The very decent Congregationalist Church of 1859, opposite the factory, is a fine example, with its peripteral Corinthian Order of columns and pilasters, and tall, elegant cupola. This church was naturally enough the first public building erected by Salt while the town itself was being constructed, and it is the most monumental of all the religious buildings in Saltaire. It was followed in the years 1863-76 by the building of baths and wash-houses, chapels, schools, almshouses and infirmary, the Club and Institute, Saltaire Park and the Sunday Schools.

Although the town is small in area, only a quarter of a mile square, it has over eight hundred houses built in terraces, with back yards containing coal stores and, originally, privies. At the rear of these terraces are long alleys giving access to the back yards for the removal of refuse and the delivery of coal, so the layout was similar to other typical nineteenth-century housing developments. Saltaire was saved from the degeneration found in larger towns by its compact size, its amenities in the form of churches, institutions and parks, and the prosperity of 'The Works'. The elevational treatment of the houses was of a much higher order than the usual pattern, for Lockwood and Mawson favoured an Italianate style, reminiscent of a very small-scale Venetian Gothic, in stone, and the quality of design and construction was excellent. The almshouses are particularly good examples of their work in Saltaire (plate 47).

The street names of Salt's model town reflect his loyalty to the sovereign and to his associates, for, apart from the expected Victoria and Albert Roads, there are Lockwood and Mawson Streets and others named after members of his large family. Walking through this pleasant, regularly planned town, the observer is struck by the quality of the housing, and by the subtle variations of design. The houses are of different sizes, as Salt displayed an astonishingly enlightened approach when he conducted surveys of the housing needs of his workers. The result was that houses were provided which suited family functions, and contained two, three or four bedrooms. Monotony of architectural treatment was thus avoided, as was rigidity of accommodation, major advantages not only over other working-class housing of the period, but indeed over many housing estates of today. Each house had a parlour, kitchen, store and cellar, in addition to the bedroom. In short, Mr Salt was a true philanthropist, as well as a practical man always with an eye to function.

In due course Salt became a Member of Parliament, and although he was a conscientious attender at the House, he was so overawed by the formality of the place that he only spoke when constituency business had to be raised, such was his shyness in the London world. He returned to Saltaire, rather disillusioned and in poor health, and at once commissioned a mausoleum to be attached to his beloved Congregationalist church. This square structure, to the south of the church, is suitably solid to commemorate its occupant.

Yet, despite the mausoleum, Salt had a lot of life, some fifteen years, in fact, left to him. He improved Saltaire in those last years, and formed a Joint Stock Company so that the firm would not be entirely in his hands. His efforts were rewarded by a baronetcy in 1869, and his arms included a crest incorporating an alpaca, with the motto *Quid Non Deo Juvante*, a suitable phrase.

The proceeds of worsted manufacture helped to build the Albert Memorial, and Salt purchased one of the largest boxes in the Albert Hall so that he could enjoy the brilliance of the spectacle, although, on his own admission, music, apart from Congregationalist hymns, was rather beyond his comprehension. In fact, although his library was vast, his reading was limited to the public prints and to religious tracts, according to his biographer.

When Sir Titus died in 1876, crape in huge quantities was draped over his statue in Bradford, and a long funeral procession wended its way from Bradford

Town Hall to the mausoleum in Saltaire. Holroyd, like Balgarnie, a Salt enthusiast, burst forth in doggerel verse to the effect that

> *Thousands mourn the loss to-day,*
> *Of the good man passed away*

and the excellent Sir Titus was laid to rest. A hefty angel, standing between Florentine pilasters carrying a suitable inscription, stands guard above his vault.

Today, 'The Works' still flourishes, but there have been changes in the town. The baths and wash-houses have been demolished, and the occupiers of the houses are no longer subject to the eagle eyes of Salt and his henchmen, who forbade the hanging of washing in the yards. Washing had to be done in the building erected for that purpose, three boilers providing facilities for the washing and drying of bodies and clothes. A pub now exists, which would not have been approved of, but the houses are being cleaned and restored to something of their original crispness. The atmosphere of Saltaire is most agreeable, and to explore its pleasant streets is an experience worth remembering. Salt and his architects succeeded in creating an aesthetically effective industrial town, large enough to provide communal and other facilities, but not likely to be strangled by excessive growth. Bradford is today practically joined to Saltaire, but the little town preserves its identity and individual character. The admirable qualities of endeavour, solidity, worthiness and humanity are reflected in its architecture.

It would be hard to name a more decent personification of the Victorian industrialist-benefactor than Sir Titus Salt, whose 'indomitable perseverance' and 'resolute will and patient toil' led to fortune, honour, and the creation of the pleasant little town that is the lasting memorial to one of the most remarkable of practical Victorians. (Plate 54.)

CHAPTER 10

Aspects of Housing

... *function*
Is smother'd in surmise, and nothing is
But what is not.

William Shakespeare

Despite the vast amount of material that has been published dealing with the Victorian age, it is a commonly held belief that Victorian buildings were 'monstrosities', 'horrors', 'inconvenient' and 'unfunctional'.

The Victorians were not the romantics and eclectics they have been imagined at all, but practical people, who designed and built to last, using the new materials and techniques of the age, and using them extremely well. They were extremely hard-headed too, and sometimes had to be jolted into reform by sudden disaster. Just as an earlier generation had been shocked by pestilence into providing for the disposal of dead bodies, sewage, and refuse, and for the purification of drinking-water, so in the 1880s the sensational Jack the Ripper murders drew attention to the appalling housing conditions of the East End, and to the lot of the social failure and outcast.

This is an interesting story, and must be told in full, for it shook the conscience of Victorian England. In the autumn of 1888, Spitalfields, once a prosperous new town laid out in the early years of the eighteenth century and occupied by Huguenot silk weavers, had declined into an area of seedy lodging-houses inhabited by the dregs of London society. Even the churchyard of Christ Church, the great building by Nicholas Hawksmoor, was known as 'itchy park' from the larger number of down-and-outs who slept there. Dorset Street was noted as the most evil street in the metropolis, and the vile-smelling courts were the haunts of robbers, prostitutes and alcoholics.

In the nineteenth century, the Flower and Dean Street area of Spitalfields declined, to become the centre of the common lodging-house district of East London. Even in the reign of William IV, Thrawl Street, Wentworth Street, and the immediate surroundings were a rabbit-warren of dormitories for the poorest population of the East End. Decaying buildings, conscienceless owners, greedy agents, appalling dirt, and abject poverty acted in concert to reduce Spitalfields to a seething, infested midden for rejected humanity. To the discomfiture of reformers, the inhabitants seemed to value the freedom the lodging-house system offered, for communal kitchens and accommodation for a few pence had attractions that higher rents, supervision, cleanliness and godliness could hardly supply, especially since alcohol, thieving, and prostitution were the bases of the local economy.

During the 1870s, the powers conferred on the Metropolitan Board of Works by the *Artisans' and Labourers' Dwellings Improvement Act* of 1875 enabled schemes for the redevelopment of the worst areas to be actively considered. In the Flower and Dean Street area alone, according to the *Survey of London*, there were 123 rooms in registered lodging-houses that contained 757 people. Such redevelopment as did take place, however, was carried out by the East End Dwellings Company and by the Four Per Cent Industrial Dwellings Company, and consisted of grim tenement blocks (plate 55). The former company was founded by a group of persons associated with the church of St Jude, while the latter was, somewhat appropriately, perhaps, the creation of Lord Rothschild specifically to house Jewish artisans.

Needless to say, these attempts to alleviate conditions were only a fleabite compared with the scale of the problem. It was the 'surgical' activities of Jack the Ripper that actually drew attention to the true state of affairs, for although the lodging-houses were subject to some system of control under an Act of Parliament of 1851, the problems of unemployment, poverty, illness, and accommodation for the very poor were hardly considered. The moral and physical wrecks who inhabited the lodging-houses were gathered together within a very small geographical area, thus they were out of sight of the more respectable members of society. The Whitechapel murders drew the spotlight of public attention to a cesspool of human degradation in a dramatic, indeed melodramatic, way.

When two Whitechapel whores were disembowelled, one in Buck's Row, and the other in Hanbury Street, only a minor stir was caused, as such events were not uncommon. When, however, the perpetrator wrote to the newspapers, to the police and to the authorities, informing them that he was going to continue his slaughter, the excitement quickened, and when he actually murdered two more prostitutes in one night, one of them in the City of London, as he had promised, the sense of outrage was complete. The murderer then wrote announcing he had eaten half of one of the kidneys of his last victim for breakfast, and enclosed the other half to prove it. Speculation as to his identity became rife, and he added pungency to the controversy as to his nationality with a little verse:

> *I'm not a butcher, nor a Yid,*
> *Nor yet a foreign skipper:*
> *I'm just your old light-hearted friend,*
> *Yours truly, Jack the Ripper.*

Since all the victims of the Ripper had been poor drabs addicted to booze, agitation grew to a tremendous pitch to improve the lot of the 'unfortunate'. Earlier, Mayhew had drawn attention to the vile conditions under which the urban poor lived, conditions of which the upper classes were patently oblivious. The Peabody Trust and the Improved Industrial Dwellings Company had provided some model dwellings for the poor, but these attempts were very small in scale (plate 56). William Booth had done valuable work with his Salvation Army, but society was not really touched to the point of radical legislation.

This could have continued indefinitely, had not Jack the Ripper struck again, leaving behind him a masterpiece in ghastliness. In a room in Miller's

Court, Dorset Street (renamed Duval Street after the murder), he killed an Irish tart named Mary or Marie Kelly, and cut her to pieces, arranging her entrails in artistic Rococo festoons all over the walls, bed and table. The publicity given in the newspapers (which unsqueamishly spared none of the details) caused such an outrage that public intervention to improve housing for the poorer classes became a matter for the national conscience, and the *Housing for the Working Classes Act* was passed in 1890, marking the first stage in housing law on a modern scale.[1]

When we consider working-class housing, it is often forgotten that the somewhat grim tenements of the East End and elsewhere were replacements of warrens of stinking cellars and rooms. The open stairs and access galleries, denounced by many, were purely functional in origin (plate 12). Staircases which were closed, constructed of timber and communal, stank to high heaven because they were used as public lavatories by tenants and by the public. An open stairwell constructed of concrete, brick and iron was easily hosed down, and was permanently ventilated. In addition, it is often forgotten that in the 1880s and 1890s, women wore heavy cumbersome clothes, so the new type of staircase was less of a hazard for the ladies as they were less likely to get their clothes filthy on a maintained, clean and open stair than on some mean internal staircase in a dark corner which once was in a self-contained house. The tenements erected in the East End at the time of the Whitechapel murders are constructed of good quality bricks, with terra-cotta dressings, and plenty of glazed bricks in situations such as stair wells. The style is generally debased Classical, with remnants of cornices and vestigial pilasters, although occasional sub-Gothic examples may be found.

The demand for urban housing in the nineteenth century was unprecedented. Much has been written about the problems of the new manufacturing towns, and the squalor in which people lived. Manchester was described by Kay, London by Mayhew, and Engels gave a monumental general picture in his *Condition of the Working Classes in England in 1844*. It is often forgotten, however, that the little terrace-houses of brick offered more substantial shelter than the rural hut. The character of rural housing was poorest in Ireland, in the Highlands of Scotland and in Wales, and the unbelievable squalor of the Irish homestead was a real and terrible fact. Often houses were built of turf with only a hole to let the smoke out, a pit in the ground outside the entrance served both as privy and midden. Neither rain nor cold was kept out, and such cabins were common until the Great Famine solved the rural overcrowding problem in Ireland. The misery of Irish country life was prolonged by the conacre[2] system, by absentee landlords, and by Irish land agents who abused their powers. Perhaps the only release from such conditions was death, or, less drastic, emigration. A certain alleviation could be obtained by the liberal use of the demon drink, notably the home-distilled variety[3] which often caused madness, blindness and death, while a remaining folk-culture gave some identity to a dismally poor people. It was not until the 1840s that the industries managed to take some of the surplus population off the land in any numbers, whereas industrialisation had begun in earnest in eighteenth-century England. The growth of industrial towns in Ireland, such as Belfast, was accelerated by the famines of the 1840s which emptied the countryside and jammed every port and town with destitute families.

The closely knit streets of Victorian Belfast give us some idea of the immense improvement of the lot of the rural poor compared with their insanitary hovels. Artisans' houses near its mills had a post-Georgian simplicity, and while they were not exactly salubrious, nor, indeed, spacious, they offered shelter to the poor, in a situation near both work and shops (plate 57). It must be remembered that at the time of their building they were situated near the open countryside. As Belfast expanded, the short-sightedness of its city fathers failed to allow for the retention of adequate open space for recreation. The inevitable legacy of the early twentieth century has been to breed generations who have no contact with their rural past, and whereas the Victorians built to solve the urgent requirements of a generation desperate for work and shelter, they had the open country to act as a safety-valve. The requirements of modern technology have eaten into the green lungs of our cities, and, although many places, notably those in the north of England, possess public parks laid out in Victorian times, the misuse of land is a great problem today.

In contrast with the little terraces of Belfast, it would be interesting to consider a fairly typical early-Victorian double-fronted house of the type leased to middle-class families. The example (plate 58) shows the plans of a house five windows wide, with classical proportions, and faced with stucco. It is fairly typical of houses erected between 1825 and 1860 in parts of London, Cheltenham, and many other towns and cities. The first fact that should be noticed is the very considerable width of such houses, usually 45 to 50ft. A large basement contained the kitchen, scullery, larder, stores, coal-sheds and housekeeper's room. The large area given over to the storage of beer and wine should be noticed, for it was not until the later years of the nineteenth century that the Temperance Movement really made its influence felt. It must also be remembered that a fairly well-to-do Victorian household consisted of a very large number of people. Apart from *pater-familias* and his spouse, there were several children, nursemaids, governesses, parlourmaids, a housekeeper, a butler, a footman or two and probably several relatives of the head of the household and his wife. These relatives were usually fading unmarried sisters or aunts and idle uncles or brothers who needed a plentiful supply of alcohol to get them through the day in order that they would be able to totter down to an immense meal before an evening of billiards or cards.

The main floor of the house was at ground-floor level, and consisted of a good-sized dining-room and drawing-room, entrance hall, staircase, butler's pantry, closets and library. The seclusion of the library should be noted, and the separate servants' stair, which remained a feature of the better type of house until fairly recently, is of interest. Since the main rooms had stately proportions and high ceilings (a necessary functional requirement, since large numbers of persons congregating in rooms use up the air quickly and cause staleness and overheating), the smaller rooms could do with lower ceilings, so an extra floor could be placed over them. Note the 'men's-rooms', boxroom and cupboard spaces on this mezzanine level.

Above there could be one, two or three floors of bedrooms disposed about the main stair. Servants slept in the attic or on the top floor, and care was taken to segregate the sexes. Lustful goings-on via the 'back stairs' were to be avoided.

Rooms were illuminated by candlelight and oil-lamps, until the advent of gas. Generally speaking, main rooms continued to be lit by candlelight, as chandeliers were particularly beautiful features of the furnishing. Gas-light was used to light the hall, stairs, and other places needing perpetual illumination. In some cases, gasoliers were provided, but the rapid deterioration of leather bindings, leather chairs, fabrics, and other decoration owing to the acidic gases emitted by burning coal-gas made gas-light in houses unpopular. The hiss, condensation, dirt and fumes made the method disagreeable, and the impracticalities of laying intestinal tubes, subject to fracture and leakage, within confined spaces were great. The arrival of electrical power was a major revolution in living habits that cannot be overstated, despite the early technical teething-troubles, and was a tremendous step forward. As gas-light in houses went out, so did spittoons, those revolting receptacles of filth, whose abolition has been a major triumph. It is not generally realised that spittoons were a normal feature of the Victorian hotel, dining-room, pub, and even living-room. The incidence of bronchitis, tuberculosis, and excess mucus and phlegm caused by the smoky atmosphere, made spitting an almost universal habit. The general education of the public to avoid this despicable activity has not only improved things aesthetically, but has obviously lessened a source of infection.

Water-closets were provided, but piped water was laid on in general to the basement and one point on each floor. Hot water was brought by servants to bedrooms for ablutions, although bathrooms were fairly common by the mid-nineteenth century. Heating was by open coal-fire, and some gas-fires were commonly provided by the 1860s.

The appearance of houses in the towns was not ignored. The careful stucco detail was an attempt to add quality to buildings, for as early as 1766 John

Gwynn stated that 'no publick edifice ought to be built with brick unless it is afterwards stucco'd, for a mere brick face in such buildings always makes a mean appearance ...'. Stucco had been used from ancient times, but in England stuccoed buildings were the exception until the mid-eighteenth century. Coade stone was a successful attempt to provide a durable material rather like stone, but it, like terra-cotta, had to be manufactured and then brought to the building site. Stucco was, of course, an *in situ* material, and was admirably suited to the enrichment of unified terraces popularised by Wyatt, Nash and the Adam brothers. By the 1850s 'Parker's Roman Cement' was the most popular variety of stucco, and is found specified on drawings by Thomson and others.

Stucco was intended to imitate stone, as speculative buildings in the towns had to be constructed at realistic prices. A stucco that was unpainted was clearly an ideal, but Roman cement was an unattractive brown-grey colour, so painting was necessary. The functional aspects of applying paint to stucco cannot be too strongly stressed, for the material when dry became covered by fine cracks, and so had to be painted to fill these minute cracks and prevent dirt and moisture entering. Unpainted stucco quickly grew a stubble of vegetation, and moisture in the cracks froze in cold weather, causing large areas of stucco to become detached. Oil paint was waterproof, and brightened up stucco work considerably.

Industrial mass-production helped in the creation of unified streetscapes during Victorian times. The spear-headed cast-iron railings, all from the same mould, will be familiar to many people, for millions of them were manufactured to protect 'areas' or light wells to basements adjacent to pavements and open spaces (plate 60). Similarly, cast-iron fireplaces, usually with white marble surrounds, could be mass-produced to add a touch of elegance to the most ordinary rooms.

All sorts of detail, apart from railings, could be manufactured by the new industrial processes. Bootscrapers, absolute necessities at a time when the surfaces of roads were not 'metalled' and therefore liable to become muddied in rainy weather, were provided at all house entrances. They were usually made of cast iron and were built into walls. Ventilators were also made of cast iron, although they are also found made of clay (plate 59).

The building illustrated has a communal entrance with a stone stair, but even so, a bootscraper is provided, and a sensible, functional approach to the provision of ventilation is adopted.

As the century progressed and Gothic, picturesque forms replaced symmetrical classicism in architectural taste, buildings tended to express their internal arrangements, and indeed it became morally obligatory to emphasise plan forms in the external form. Positions of staircases were made clear in elevational treatment, and the location of principal rooms may be easily discerned in Victorian houses, even if the concessions to Gothic detail are minimal. A charming little red-brick villa in Mistley, Essex, has been chosen for the final illustration (plate 61). The influence of Butterfield and others is clearly revealed by the bands of dark and light bricks, by the relieving arches, by the decorative *paterae*, and by the splayed jambs. The elaborate brick eaves and the finely detailed lintels are clearly a result of the obsessional attention to architectural craftsmanship established at the height of the Gothic Revival. The disposition of the main rooms is clearly seen, and there is no doubt where the door is situated. The romantic silhouette and little pyramidal spirelet over the entrance are a direct result of an approach to architectural design very different from that of thirty years before. It is the miniature of some North Oxford fantasy. It should be noted, however, that, for all the picturesque effects and romantic appearance, the amount of materials needing maintenance is minimal. Nearly all the outside of the house is built of bricks or slates. The parts which require painting every few years are the gutters and downpipes (cast iron), window sashes and frames (timber), door (timber), and door-furniture (iron). Without vast areas of stucco requiring regular painting, this is a cheap building to maintain, and therefore functional. The Mistley house is not too far removed either in massing or style from Philip Webb's 'Red House' that he built for William Morris, and indeed Victorian functional architecture in housing perhaps reached its culmination with the Arts and Crafts movement. The simplicity and practicality of fittings and furnishings by Voysey and Gimson, for example, both work and are supremely satisfactory aesthetically.

Yet the Arts and Crafts movement and the design of villas were far removed from the realities of working-class housing. The tenements of Peabody, the Four Per Cent Industrial Dwellings Company, and the open stair wells first shown at the 1851 exhibition represented the realities of mass-housing. Private philanthropy was only replaced by public authority housing after Jack the Ripper's adventures in 1888. It is not insignificant that the LCC was founded in 1889, and it was responsible for the building of the earliest municipal and working-class flats in England.

Victorian architecture is fascinating. It is quite unlike any architecture before it, because it had to respond to new functional needs. We look at a building such as a Bassett Keeling church with a cloudy eye today. We can enjoy the stencilled patterns, the cast-iron columns, and the superbly functional joinery. We tend to forget, however, that the building was once bursting at the seams with large congregations, and a great deal of height was necessary to avoid overheating, excessively stale air, or simply a concentrated stench of human bodies. St Pancras Station Hotel looks marvellous from Percy Circus, and it appears dreamily romantic. To imagine it raw, red, and new, set among the muddy streets with

H

open fields in the distance and horse-drawn vehicles everywhere, requires an effort of our imaginations.

We can view Wormwood Scrubs from the railway line leaving Paddington. It requires an equivalent jump of our imaginations to see convict labour burning the bricks, constructing the buildings and working to plans drawn up by the soldier Du Cane.

The Victorian age responded to the necessities of its own time. It adopted a realistic, imaginative and functional approach to design and constructional problems.

Our own times, hedged about by bureaucracy, paperwork and lack of any appreciation of what constitutes a working environment, could take note and learn from a braver, bolder and, for all its faults, more exciting period.

Notes to this chapter are on page 119

References

CHAPTER ONE   An Introduction (pp13-20)

See General Bibliography

CHAPTER TWO   New Materials and New Ideas (pp21-33)

1 Quoted in Clark, Kenneth. *The Gothic Revival. An Essay in the History of Taste* (Harmondsworth 1964)
2 Jordan, Robert Furneaux. *Victorian Architecture* (Harmondsworth 1966), 89
3 Ibid
4 See Thompson, Paul. *William Butterfield* (1971)
5 Pevsner, Nikolaus. *Pioneers of Modern Design* (1960), 132
6 Chadwick, George F. *The Works of Sir Joseph Paxton 1803-1865* (1961)
7 Honikman, Basil. 'The Early Days of Industrialised Buildings', *Systems Building and Design* (April 1968)
8 Curl, James Stevens. 'Manchester's Victorian Heritage', *Country Life* (26 February 1970)
9 I am indebted to Mr John Hix for this information
10 Goodhart-Rendel, H. S. 'Brompton, London's Art Quarter', *RIBA Journal* (January 1956)
11 Rasmussen, Steen Eiler. *London, the Unique City* (Harmondsworth 1960), 193-4
12 Knight, Charles (ed). Revised and corrected by Walford, E. *London*, vol 6 (1841-4 and many later editions), 320
13 Lee, Charles E. 'St Pancras Station, 1868-1968', *The Railway Magazine* (September, October 1968)

14 Ibid

15 From *The Journal of Design* (1851), quoted by Nikolaus Pevsner in *Pioneers of Modern Design* (Harmondsworth 1960), 133

16 Meeks, C. L. V. *The Railroad Station* (Yale and London 1956)

17 Ruskin, John. *The Seven Lamps of Architecture* (Orpington 1889), 35

18 Curl. *The Victorian Celebration of Death* (Newton Abbot 1972). See also Curl. 'Highgate: A Great Victorian Cemetery', *RIBA Journal* (April 1968)

19 Young, G. M. *Early Victorian England* (London, New York and Toronto 1951), vol 1, 201-6

20 See Walford, Edward. *Old and New London* (London, Paris and New York 1887) vol 5

21 Curl. *The Victorian Celebration of Death* (Newton Abbot 1972), 147-54, for further information on Haywood as a designer of cemeteries. See also Boase, Frederic. *Modern English Biography, containing many thousand concise memoirs of persons who have died between the years 1851-1900* (1965)

22 Goodhart-Rendel, H. S. 'Victorian Public Buildings'. Text of a lecture given at the Victoria and Albert Museum in 1952, and published in Ferriday, Peter (ed), *Victorian Architecture* (1963)

23 Curl, James Stevens. 'Manchester's Victorian Heritage', *Country Life* (26 February 1970)

CHAPTER THREE   Symbols, Cathedrals and Churches (pp35-44)

1 Curl, James Stevens. *European Cities and Society. The Influence of Political Climate on Town Design* (1970)

2 Holt, Elizabeth G. (ed). *A Documentary History of Art*, vol 1 (New York 1957), 18

3 Adams, Henry. *Mont Saint-Michel and Chartres* (New York 1959), 67

4 Curl. Op cit, 23-43

5 Douglas, Norman. *Old Calabria* (Harmondsworth 1962), 322

6 Curl. Op cit, 6-7
  von Franz, M-L. and Jung, C. G. (ed). *Man and His Symbols* (1964)

7 Howard, Ebenezer. *Tomorrow: A Peaceful Path to Real Reform* (1898)

8 Giedion, Sigfried. *The Eternal Present* (New York and London 1962), vol 1, 125

9 Curl. 'Symbolism and the Springs of creative invention', *The Architect*, April 1971

10 Eastlake, Charles L. *A History of the Gothic Revival* (Crook, J. Mordaunt, ed) (Leicester and New York 1970), 1

11 Burckhardt, Jacob. *The Civilisation of the Renaissance in Italy* (Middlemore, S. G. C., tr) (Vienna and London 1937)

12 Eastlake, Charles L. Op cit, 1

13 Clark, Kenneth. *The Gothic Revival. An Essay in the History of Taste*

14 Pugin, A. W. N. *Contrasts, or a Parallel between the Noble Edifices of the Fourteenth and Fifteenth Centuries and Similar Buildings of the Present Day* (1836)

15 Feriday, Peter (ed).*Victorian Architecture* (1963), 143

CHAPTER FOUR   An Inventive Architect, or, Acrobatic Gothic, Freely Treated (pp45-55)

1 Ricardo, Halsey. Obituary of J. F. Bentley in *The Architectural Review*

2 His death certificate gives his first name as 'Enock'

3 *The Builder* (20 November 1886), 753

4 *The Builder* (22 October 1864), 771-2

5 Hollingshead, John. *Gaiety Chronicles* (1898)

6 & 7 Ibid

8 *The Builder* (20 November 1886), 753

9 *The Times* (17 January 1865), 9, col 6

10 *The Times* (19 July 1866), 10, col e

11 *The Times* (18 March 1865), 13, col e

12 *The Builder* (1 November 1862), 790, and CC File 26098

13 Ibid, 790

14 *The Building News* (13 August 1869), 121

15 *The Building News* (29 January 1864), 85

16 Pepperell, William: *The Church Index* (1872), 33-4

17 *The Building News* (22 July 1864), 560

18 *The Builder* (11 August 1866), 602

19 I am indebted to the Reverend P. M. Leach for access to the church and permission to measure it

20 *The British Architect* (12 October 1883), 172

21 *The Builder* (21 June 1884), 912

22 Death certificates in Somerset House, and Abney Park Cemetery Records

23 I am grateful to Dove Brothers, of Islington, who built many of Keeling's designs, for access to material in the possession of the firm

24 I am indebted to Mr John J. Sambrook who collaborated with me in the production of this chapter. See our 'Gothic Freely Treated' in *The Architect*, August 1972

CHAPTER FIVE   New Technology and Victorian Traffic Relief (pp57-67)

1 Curl, James Stevens. 'The Townscape of Manningtree and Mistley', *Town and Country Planning* (September 1970)
2 Routledge, Robert. *Discoveries and Inventions of the Nineteenth Century* (1881), 236-44

CHAPTER SIX   Gin Palaces (pp69-76)

1 Curl, James Stevens 'Victoriana in Ulster Pubs', *Country Life* (15 May 1969)
2 Curl. *The Victorian Celebration of Death*
   Curl. 'Highgate', *RIBA Journal* (April 1968)
3 Geary, Stephen. *Cemetery Designs for Tombs and Cenotaphs* (1840)
4 Curl. *European Cities and Society*, 131, 144
5 Curl. 'The Vanished Gin Palaces', *Country Life* (22 June 1972)

CHAPTER SEVEN   Prisons and Hospitals (pp77-88)

1 Rosenau, Helen. *Social Purpose in Architecture. Paris and London Compared, 1760-1800* (1970), 78
2 Howard, J. *An Account of the Principal Lazarettos in Europe* (1789)
3 Howard, J. *The State of the Prisons in England and Wales* (Warrington 1784)
4 Apart from the papers in the possession of Mr A. W. Pullan, the information on Sir Edmund Du Cane was obtained from *The Dictionary of National Biography*. The details concerning Wormwood Scrubs Prison were abstracted from Du Cane, Colonel Sir Edmund F., KCB, RE, *A Description of Wormwood Scrubs Prison with An Account of the Circumstances attending its Erection* (1887)
5 Tenon, J. R. *Mémoires sur les hôpitaux de Paris* (Paris 1788)
6 Howard. *The State of the Prisons in England and Wales*
7 Walford, Edward. *Old and New London : A Narrative of its History, its People, and its Places* (nd), 419-22
8 *The Builder* (16 January 1904), 64
9 *The Builder* (12 July 1879), 785
10 *The Builder* (25 June 1881), 792
11 *The Builder* (19 March 1881), 354-5
12 Ibid
13 *The Builder* (25 June 1881), 792

14 See also *The Builder* (26 March 1881), 392; (11 November 1882), 639; (16 June 1883), 834; (5 July 1884), 41; (26 July 1884), 122; (23 April 1887), 627; (1 March 1890), 163; (1 March 1879), 241; (15 March 1879), 297; (12 April 1879), 414; (12 July 1879), 785; (22 May 1880), 651

CHAPTER EIGHT   The Search for Durable Materials and Healthier Cities
                 (pp89-98)

 1 Curl, James Stevens. 'The Challenge of Clerkenwell', *Country Life* (8/22 April 1971)
 2 Jacob, Ernest. *Notes on the Ventilation and Warming* . . . etc (1894)
 3 Ricardo, Halsey. 'Of Colour in the Architecture of Cities', *Art and Life, and the Building and Decoration of Cities* (1897)
 4 Ibid, 247
 5 Ibid, 259
 6 Ricardo, Halsey. *The Builder* (7 July 1894)
 7 Ibid
 8 Curl. *European Cities and Society*, 134-5
 9 Rolt, L. T. C. *Victorian Engineering* (1970), 140-3
10 Ibid, 141
11 Ibid, 144
12 See *The Illustrated London News* (April 1865), and Walford's *Old and New London* for contemporary notices
13 Alison, Archibald. *Essays on the Nature and Principles of Taste* (Edinburgh 1811), 24-5
14 Loudon, John Claudius. *Encyclopaedia of Cottage, Farm and Villa Architecture* (edition of 1846 enlarged by Mrs Jane Loudon), 1105-24
15 Ibid
16 Ibid
17 Ibid
18 Ibid
19 Loudon, John Claudius. *On the laying out, planting, and managing of Cemeteries; and on the Improvement of Churchyards* (1843)
20 Curl. *The Victorian Celebration of Death*

CHAPTER TEN   Aspects of Housing (pp 105-14)
 1 Curl. *European Cities and Society*, 136-8
 2 Short-term rent of eleven months. See Mogey, J. *Rural Life in Northern Ireland* (1947), 19, 38, 43, 157, 176-81
 3 See *The North British Mail* (20 June 1849)

General Bibliography

Adams, Henry. *Mont Saint-Michel and Chartres* (New York 1959)

Adshead, J. *Prisons and Prisoners* (1845)

Alison, Archibald, *Essays on the Nature and Principles of Taste* (Edinburgh 1811)

Alsop, B. *The Late Sir Titus Salt, Bart, Founder of Saltaire* (Saltaire 1878)

Armytage, W. H. G. *A Social History of Engineering* (1961)

Balgarnie, R. *Sir Titus Salt, His Life and Lessons* (1877)

Barman, Christian. *An Introduction to Railway Architecture* (1950)

Benevolo, Leonardo (Lantry, Judith, tr). *The Origins of Modern Town Planning* (1967)

Bentham, J. *Panopticon; or, The Inspection House* ... (1791)

Binny, J. See Mayhew, H.

Boase, Frederic. *Modern English Biography, containing many thousand concise memoirs of persons who have died between the years 1851-1900* (1965)

Briggs, Asa. *Victorian Cities* (Harmondsworth 1968)

British Architect, The. See Chapter Notes

Buckingham, James S. *National Evils and Practical Remedies, with the Plan of a Model Town* (1849)

Builder, The. See Chapter Notes

Building News, The. See Chapter Notes

Burckhardt, Jacob (Middlemore, S. G. C., tr). *The Civilization of the Renaissance in Italy* (Vienna and London 1937)

Chadwick, Sir Edwin. *A Supplementary Report to Her Majesty's Secretary of State for the Home Department from the Poor Law Commissioners on the Results of a Special Inquiry into the Practice of Interment in Towns* (1843)

Chadwick, George F. *The Works of Sir Joseph Paxton 1803-1865* (1961)

Clark, Kenneth. *The Gothic Revival. An Essay in the History of Taste*

(Harmondsworth 1964)

Clarke, Basil F. L. *Church Builders of the Nineteenth Century* (Newton Abbot 1969)

Colvin, H. M. *A Biographical Dictionary of English Architects 1660-1840* (1954)

Coleman, Terry. *The Railway Navvies* (Harmondsworth 1968)

Crook, J. Mordaunt. See Eastlake, Charles L.

Croome, Desmond. See Jackson, Alan A.

Cudworth, William. *Saltaire, A Sketch History* (Saltaire 1895)

Curl, James Stevens. *European Cities and Society. A Study of the Influence of Political Climate on Town Design* (1970 and 1972)

    'Manchester's Victorian Heritage', *Country Life* (26 February 1970)

    'Highgate: A Great Victorian Cemetery', *RIBA Journal* (April 1968)

    'Symbolism and the Springs of Creative Intention', *The Architect* (April 1971)

    'The Townscape of Manningtree and Mistley', *Town and Country Planning* (September 1970)

    The Victorian Celebration of Death (Newton Abbot 1972)

    'The Victorians Considered as Functionalists', *RIBA Journal* (January 1969)

    'Victoriana in Ulster Pubs', *Country Life* (15 May 1969)

    'The Challenge of Clerkenwell', *Country Life* (8 and 22 April 1971)

    'A Victorian Model Town', *Country Life* (9 March 1972)

    'The Vanished Gin Palaces', *Country Life* (22 June 1972)

    (with John Sambrook) 'Gothic Freely Treated. A Look at the Career of E. Bassett Keeling', *The Architect* (August 1972)

Dainton, C. *The Story of England's Hospitals* (1961)

Derry, T. K. and Williams, T. I. *A Short History of Technology* (Oxford 1960)

Dimier, L. *L'Hôtel des Invalides* (Paris 1910)

Dodds, Gordon. See Wilkes, Lyall

Douglas, Norman. *Old Calabria* (Harmondsworth 1962)

Du Cane, Colonel Sir Edmund F. *A Description of Wormwood Scrubs Prison with an Account of the Circumstances Attending Its Erection* (1887)

Eastlake, Charles L. (Crook, J. Mordaunt, ed). *A History of the Gothic Revival* (Leicester and New York 1970)

Ellis, Hamilton. *British Railway History* (1954 and 1959)

Elmes, J. *Hints for the Improvement of Prisons, etc* (1817)

Engels, F. (Wischnewetzky, tr). *The Condition of the Working Classes in England in 1844* (1892)

Fairbairn, William. *On the Application of Cast and Wrought Iron to Building Purposes* (1857)

Fergusson, J. *History of Architecture* (1869)

Ferriday, Peter (ed). *Victorian Architecture* (1963)

Franz, M-L. von and Jung, C. G. (ed). *Man and His Symbols* (1964)

Gale, W. K. V. *The Black Country Iron Industry* (1966)

Geary, Stephen. *Cemetery Designs for Tombs and Cenotaphs* (1840)

Giedion, Sigfried. *The Eternal Present* (New York and London 1962)

Goodhart-Rendel, H. S. 'Brompton, London's Art Quarter', *RIBA Journal* (January 1956)

　'Victorian Public Buildings', Text of a lecture given at The Victoria and Albert Museum in 1952, and published in Ferriday, Peter (ed), *Victorian Architecture* (1963)

　English Architecture since the Regency (1953)

Halstead, P. E. 'The Early History of Portland Cement', *Newcomen Society Transactions*, vol 34 (1961-2)

Hamilton, S. B. 'Sixty Glorious Years. The Impact of Engineering on Society in the Reign of Queen Victoria', *Newcomen Society Transactions*, vol 31 (1957-9)

Hitchcock, H.-R. *Early Victorian Architecture in Britain* (1954)

Hobhouse, Christopher. *1851 and the Crystal Palace* (1950)

Hollingshead, John. *Gaiety Chronicles* (1898)

Holroyd, Abraham. *Saltaire and Its Founder* (Saltaire 1871)

Holt, Elizabeth G. (ed). *A Documentary History of Art* (New York 1957)

Honikman, Basil. 'The Early Days of Industrialised Building', *Systems, Building and Design* (April 1968)

Howard, Ebenezer. *Tomorrow : A Peaceful Path to Real Reform* (1898)

Howard, J. *An Account of the Principal Lazarettos in Europe* (1789)

　The State of the Prisons in England and Wales (Warrington 1784)

Illustrated London News, The. See Chapter Notes

Jackson, Alan A. and Croome, Desmond. *Rails through the Clay—A History of London's Tube Railways* (1962)

Jacob, Ernest. *Notes on the Ventilation and Warming . . . etc* (1894)

Jones, K. *Lunacy, Law and Conscience, 1744-1845* (1955)

Jordan, Robert Furneaux. *Victorian Architecture* (Harmondsworth 1966)

Jung, C. G. See Franz, M-L. von

Kerr, R. *The Gentleman's House* (1869)

Klingender, Francis D. *Art and the Industrial Revolution* (1968)

Knight, Charles (ed) (revised and corrected by Walford, E.). *London*, vol 6 (1841-4, and many later editions)

Lantry, Judith. See Benevolo, Leonardo

Lee, Charles E. 'St Pancras Station, 1868-1968', *The Railway Magazine* (September/October 1968)

Lethaby, W. *Architecture* (1911)
    Form in Civilization (1922)
Lilley, S. *Men, Machines and History* (1948)
Loudon, John Claudius. *Encyclopaedia of Cottage, Farm and Villa Architecture*
    (edition of 1846, enlarged by Mrs Jane Loudon)
        On the laying out, planting, and managing of Cemeteries; and on the
        Improvement of Churchyards (1843)
McCracken, Eileen. *The Palm House and Botanic Garden, Belfast* (Belfast 1971)
MacDermot, E. T. *History of the Great Western Railway* (1927 and 1931)
McGonagall, William. *Poetic Gems* (Dundee 1970)
Mannheim, H. *Pioneers in Criminology* (1960)
Marquet-Vasselot, L. A. A. *Examen historique et critique des diverses Théories*
    Pénitentaires, etc (Lille 1835)
Mayhew, Henry (Quennell, P., ed). *London's Underworld* (1950)
Mayhew, H. and Binny, J. *The Criminal Prisons of London and Scenes of Prison*
    Life (1862)
Meeks, C. L. V. *The Railroad Station* (Yale and London 1956)
Middlebrook, S. *Newcastle-upon-Tyne. Its Growth and Achievement* (New-
    castle 1950)
Middlemore, S. G. C. See Burckhardt, Jacob
Mogey, J. *Rural Life in Northern Ireland* (1947)
Moreau-Christophe, L.-M. *De la réforme des prisons en France*, etc (Paris 1838)
Morris, William. *Hopes and Fears for Art* and *Lectures on Art and Industry*
    in the *Collected Works* (1910)
North British Mail, The. See Chapter Notes
Owen, Robert. *A New View of Society* (1818)
Pepperell, William. *The Church Index* (1872)
Pevsner, Nikolaus. *Pioneers of Modern Design* (Harmondsworth 1960)
Phillips, L. March. *Works of Man* (1913)
    Form and Colour (1915)
Pike, E. Royston. *Human Documents of the Industrial Revolution* (1966)
Pugin, A. W. N. *Contrasts, or a Parallel between the Noble Edifices of the*
    Fourteenth and Fifteenth Centuries and Similar Buildings of the Present Day
    (1836)
Quennell, P. See Mayhew, Henry
Raistrick, Arthur. *Quakers in Science and Industry* (Newton Abbot 1968)
Rasmussen, Steen Eiler. *London, the Unique City* (Harmondsworth 1960)
Reese, J. M. *The Royal Naval Hospital, Plymouth, 1762-1962* (nd)
Ricardo, Halsey. 'Of Colour in the Architecture of Cities', *Art and Life, and the*
    Building and Decoration of Cities (1897)

Rolt, L. T. C. *Victorian Engineering* (1970)
  Great Engineers (1962)
  Isambard Kingdom Brunel (1957)
  George and Robert Stephenson (1960)

Rosenau, Helen. *Social Purpose in Architecture. Paris and London Compared, 1760-1800* (1970)

Routledge, Robert. *Discoveries and Inventions of the Nineteenth Century* (1881)

Ruskin, John. *The Seven Lamps of Architecture* (Orpington 1889)

Simmons, Jack. *The Railways of Britain* (1961)

Stewart, Cecil. *A Prospect of Cities* (1952)

Sutherland, R. J. M. 'The Introduction of Structural Wrought Iron', *Newcomen Society Transactions*, vol 36 (1963-4)

Symons, Leslie (ed). *Land Use in Northern Ireland*, part of the Land Utilization Survey of Northern Ireland (1963)

Tenon, J. R. *Mémoires sur les hôpitaux de Paris* (Paris 1788)

Thompson, Paul. *William Butterfield* (1971)

Toynbee, Arnold (ed). *Cities of Destiny* (1967)

Victoria and Albert Museum. *The Great Exhibition of 1851*, a commemorative album (1950)

Walford, Edward. *Old and New London : A Narrative of Its History, Its People, and Its Places* (nd)
    See also Knight, Charles

Wilkes, Lyall and Dodds, Gordon. *Tyneside Classical. The Newcsastle of Grainger, Dobson and Clayton* (1964)

Williams, T. I. See Derry, T. K.

Wischnewetzky. See Engels, F.

Young, G. M. *Early Victorian England* (London, New York and Toronto 1951)

Index

Plate numbers are indicated in italics